WHAT IT'S REALLY LIKE

STORIES & ARTIFACTS FROM TEACHERS AROUND THE COUNTRY

JANE MORRIS

TRUTH BE TOLD PUBLISHING

Truth Be Told Publishing

ISBN: 978-0-578-66808-6

FOR M,

Always for you

OTHER BOOKS BY JANE MORRIS

Teacher Misery: Helicopter Parents, Special Snowflakes & Other Bullshit

More Teacher Misery: Nutjob Teachers, Torturous Training & Even More Bullshit

Crap My Students Make

2019-2020 Teacher Planner:
A Teacher Misery Creation

Laugh at Almost Everything:
A Teacher Misery Quote Collection
Coming soon!

(2020-2021 Planner coming soon!)

CONTENTS

Untitled	xiii
Preface	xvii
1. A Simple Request	1
2. Shit Students Say	3
3. An Email from Your Student, Cookie Monster	8
4. Popsicle Disservice	9
5. Trash Talk	11
6. The Dish I Lived In	14
7. Mommy's Little Playboy	15
8. It Wasn't Perfume	16
9. Venting Session	19
10. The Desk Humper in Question	21
11. The World's Shittiest Gifts	22
12. An Unforgettable First Day	28
13. What is this Sorcery?	30
14. Everyone Deserves to Feel Special	32
15. A Problem with No Solution	34
16. Do Not Email That Picture!	35
17. So Good but So Bad but So Good	37
18. Shit in the Vending Machine, Etc.	39
19. It's Called Life	41
20. Shit Show	43
21. Supportive Stranger	45
22. Shame	46
23. Maybe We Go To The Same Therapist!	50
24. How to Get Free Tutoring	51
25. A New Perspective	53
26. I'll Always Wonder	54
27. All is Forgiven	57
28. Not a Priority	58

29. I'm Afraid that's Your Job! 61
30. You Made It! But... 62
31. Please Extend My Warmest Congratulations 65
32. An Intro to Public School 66
33. Completely Understandable 67
34. Pet Cemetery in my Locker 68
35. Keep it Fresh 69
36. A Brief Interruption 70
37. Can't Get Nuttin Past Her! 72
38. Boys Pee Outside 73
39. Enthused! 75
40. One Barbie Short 76
41. Payment Request from Former Student 77
42. Magic Wand 78
43. Happy to be of Service 79
44. Hey! Teacher! Leave Those Frogs Alone! 80
45. TF Going on Bruh 82
46. Grandpa is Dead, See? 83
47. You Need a Snickers Bar 85
48. Whose Eye is This? 86
49. OK Then! 87
50. Two I'll Never Forget 88
51. Excuse me While I File This Restraining Order 92
52. Get Over Yourself 93
53. A Lifestyle Choice 96
54. Who Raises Them 98
55. Who Raises Them Part 2 101
56. Significant Feedback 108
57. Oh Shitballs 109
58. Saving my Daughter from Math 111
59. Call 911! My Daughter Lost a Tooth! 112
60. Like a Dog who Sees a Squirrel 114
61. Attack of the Vibrating Backpack 115
62. Your Stupid Breastmilk 117
63. Chasing Gunther 119
64. My Kid Sucks. Can He Be Excused for That? 122

65. Life is but a Dream 123
66. Thanks but No Thanks 124
67. Floyd's Little Discovery 125
68. Happy to Help 127
69. Don't Mess with Mom 128
70. Aye Bro 130
71. Rules and Regulations 131
72. That's a High Bar 132
73. A More Loving Teacher 133
74. It's Annoying 136
75. A Sudden Realization 137
76. But Did You Die? 138
77. Caution: Unstable Parent Behind the Wheel 142
78. Phantom Poopers Across the Nation 144
79. Spiritual Activity 146
80. A Horrible, Inaccurate Gift 148
81. It Takes a Machete 149
82. You Hate Our School? Publicly Lying About It 151
   Will Help!
83. Meaningful Feedback 152
84. Purposeful Peasants 157
85. Bus Driver Tells Kids to Go Fuck Themselves 158
86. I Did Not Like It 162
87. Get on that Skype! 163
88. Demon Book Selection 164
89. Toilet Seats and Other Creative Hall Passes 165
90. Just Stay in Your Lane 168
91. An Ominous Message from Your Principal 171
92. Imaginary Friend 172
93. Don't Tell My Daughter I'm an Asshole! 174
94. My Eyebrows Hurt and Other Medical 175
   Emergencies
95. Because, Ya Know, Buttholes 179
96. Asking Too Much 181
97. How to Kill Imaginary Chickens 182

98. Animal Corpses and Other Weird Shit Kids Bring to School   184

99. What Did You Think Your Salary Was For?   188

100. Sometimes It Gets In   189

101. Interesting Mix of Topics   191

102. Are You A Professional?   192

103. The Interlopers   196

104. Take My Word for It, Please   199

105. Correct Your Tone   201

106. Fun is a Crime   203

107. Honest Report Card Comments   206

108. TMI   210

109. A Love Letter of Sorts   212

110. Due Process   213

111. Shit Administrators Say   215

112. Expert Pudding Eater   220

113. A Glimmer   222

114. 2000, 2010, 2020   224

115. Just a Little Leak   227

116. #BITCHBYE   229

117. Let it Go   230

118. Know Your No's and Rolls!   232

119. Private Does Not Mean Anonymous   233

120. Privilege to Pee   234

121. Okay Bitch!   237

122. If Only This Car Would Hit Me   238

123. These Updates are Disgusting   240

124. Give Me the Sausage   242

125. Personal Note   244

126. Well That Escalated Quickly!   245

127. A Smile that Doesn't Waver   247

128. Sorry   249

129. A Tiny Fucking House   250

130. Creative Parenting Done Right   252

131. Boys Will be Boys and Other Horseshit   254

132. Morning Cocktail   264

133. Shit in the Lunch Bucket		266
134. You Teachers are like Personal Assistants, Right?		270
135. Why No One Wants to be Pep Squad Advisor		271
136. Irresponsible		274
137. Parents Who Overshare		276
138. A Sopping Wet Surprise		280
139. This Park Ain't for Punks!		285
140. Make Room for That!		286
141. What is Teaching Really Like?		288
142. Funny You Should Mention the Word UNCOMFORTABLE		293
143. Pink Car		294
144. Mom Needs a Dictionary		297
145. Raw Coconuts		298
146. Waldo's Dad Needs Gas Money		300
147. My Student Vampirina		301
148. You Ruined Her Childhood		303
149. I Say a Little Prayer for You		305
150. Flipping Students the Bird		307
151. Shit Parents Say		309
152. Commitment		313
Contain this Shit!		315
Thank you		339
Acknowledgements		341
Notes		343
About the Author		345

*Note: Everything in this book is true,
as far as I know.
Names have been changed to protect identities.*

*You might find some of it hard to believe,
but if you are a teacher,
you'll know in your bones it's real.*

The ability to laugh at life is right at the top, with love and communication, in the hierarchy of our needs. Humor has much to do with pain; it exaggerates the anxieties and absurdities we feel, so that we gain distance and through laughter, relief.

— **SARA DAVIDSON**

PREFACE

J. MORRIS

I was done. True, I had said that I was done many times before, but this time felt different.

I'd had bad classes before, with kids who seemed to get a kick out of trying to break me down. But I never had an administration who *supported* the misbehaved kids, validated every outrageous complaint they had, and blamed me entirely for their awful behavior.

"This is it!" I screamed into my phone. "I'm done! And don't try to talk me out of it! I am smart and capable and I can find another job! I can't do this anymore!"

"Okay," my husband said calmly, knowing that if I detected any emotion in his voice other than complete support, it would mean doom. "You don't need to do it anymore if you don't want to. We will figure it out. It is going to be okay." He knew the perfect response because we had been through this before. He learned the hard way that trying to point out that this little outburst was seasonal for me, and that I would get over it in a few weeks, only made the situation much, *much* worse. "Good! *Because I really am done this time!*"

I tried to get through the rest of the day. I knew that if I just walked out and didn't come back, I would ruin other future opportunities for myself, even if they weren't in teaching. Teachers who suddenly resign, with no reason other than "I just can't take it anymore!" were seen as weak. They broke their contract, which was like breaking a cosmic law. Teachers who resign in the middle of the year weren't to be trusted. The rest of the world does not see this the way the educational world does, I have learned. Other people and employers will even respect the fact that you refused to be abused any longer and put your own mental health first. But they brainwash you about a lot of things to keep you in your place, and it works.

Just get through the last class. That was all I had to do. I was not coming back, but I needed to finish out the day, at least. My last class of the day was rowdy, as kids often get at the end of the day, but they were sweet kids and they meant no harm. If I didn't have to get them to listen and produce work, we would have had a great time. They were fun and *funny*, I just couldn't really get them to shut up for very long. I announced that it was time for them to put their things away and prepare for their little five-question reading quiz, the one I had talked about every day for two weeks (They had two weeks to read 25 pages, but they were lazy as fuck.) They immediately started to push back, as kids often do.

"What quiz!"

"You never told us about a quiz!"

"I didn't have time to read!"

"Can it be open-book?"

"I read it two weeks ago, but I can't remember anything!"

"It's not fair!"

A group of the more spirited ones surrounded me and continued their badgering.

This was their typical crap. They usually tried to play this little game just to see if I would somehow give in. But this time, I was so fragile that it just seemed like too much. I sat down in my chair, and I started to cry. Once I started, I couldn't stop. Out it all came, and the room went quiet. The kids who stood near me slowly backed away.

"Are you okay?"

"We're sorry! We'll just take the quiz!" one called out.

"It's okay, Ms. Morris!"

But I couldn't pull it back. I went into the hall and grabbed a sub who was passing by and asked her to watch my class. She saw the state I was in and immediately agreed. I ran to the bathroom, sat down on the floor, and continued crying until the bell rang and the day was over.

Let me back up for a minute. *"How bad could that other class have been?"* you might be thinking. It does seem like an overreaction to fall apart the way I did, doesn't it? Allow me to tell you a little bit more about it.

It was my 15th year. I had seen a lot and dealt with a lot (if you've read my other books, then you know just how much I had dealt with.) I had cried in class once or twice before and had quit in my mind, and to my family, probably a dozen times. But this was different. I was used to having an administration and coworkers who had the attitude of, "If those kids are fucking with you, we will handle it together. We're a team. Let's go!" We comforted each other and most importantly, we *validated* each other. It's incredible just how far the words "I've been there, and it's not your fault" can go. When I've had poorly behaved kids, the head of my department, or an assistant principal, would pull them out of class and conference with them, with or without my presence (whatever I preferred.) I've had coworkers confront entire classes for me, and I've done the same for them. We got to the root of the problem in almost every situation together.

In this new school I had found myself in, everything was our fault, and the kids could do no wrong. And kids, as perceptive and manipulative as they can be, knew they had the power. It caused complete chaos. And it broke the teachers down like nothing I had ever seen.

A group of kids in this one class, in particular, came in with their minds made up about my class and me from day one. I'll spare you the details, I'm sure you can imagine what the behavior was like. After two weeks I was ready for backup. I had tried contacting parents, and speaking to each kid individually, which only seemed to make matters worse. I almost never ask administration for help, because I know they can see it as bothersome, but I was desperate. I asked the new assistant principal to come and speak to my class about their behavior. "There are a lot of well-behaved kids in this class who are suffering because of the others," I explained. "I am hoping that a strong message from administration about behavioral expectations and consequences will help."

"Sure, no problem," he responded. "I'll see you then."

I started class with a little introduction about why the assistant principal was there to speak with them, and I moved aside.

"I can tell that a lot of you are unhappy in this class," he said. "Can anyone tell me why?"

This was not what I was expecting, but he was a young, new administrator, and I figured he was using some new strategy to make the class feel comfortable. No one answered.

"Raise your hand if you like this class," he said. Half of the class raised their hands, some sat there with a blank look on their faces, a few were on their phones, and the ones who hated me sat with their arms crossed, looking angry. "Raise your hand if you *don't* like this class," he continued. "Who gives a shit if they *like* the class?" I thought. They don't have to *like* it, but they do have to act like human beings and be respectful. The angry group proudly raised their hands. "Okay, can you tell me why you feel that way?" he said. No one answered.

"Ms. Morris," he said. "Can you come here?" I walked over to him, and he whispered into my ear, "Can you wait in the hallway for a few minutes?"

"Sure," I responded. This was strange but I did as I was asked and waited in the hallway next to the door. Before the door had even closed completely, a student yelled out, "I hate that bitch!"

And so began a very inappropriate debate between the half of the class who tried to stand up for me and the small group that hated me. It lasted almost 30 minutes. From what I did hear, the kids who hated me used curse words the entire time while describing their feelings about me, and the assistant principal never once told them to stop. He validated everything they were saying. "She's a great teacher!" one girl yelled. "They don't listen!"

"She's *not* a great teacher!" one responded. "I haven't learned *shit*!"

"Well, that's because you are always talking and running around the room!"

"I asked for help, and she won't help me! She's a bitch!" another said.

"That's not true," another chimed in. "She tries to help you, but you won't let her!"

I couldn't take it anymore. All he did was try to moderate the debate. Never once did he tell them that their language was inappropriate or that it didn't matter how they felt about me, they still needed to be respectful. I slumped down to the floor and tried to block this all out, but I was shaking with anger. Other teachers walked by and asked me what was going on. When I told them what was happening they all thought it was strange. After quite a while, he stuck his head out and said, "You can come back in now."

"I don't feel comfortable coming back in after that," I said, which was true. "Okay, you can stay out here then," he responded. The bell rang soon after and I stood up by the door. The angry kids whisked by me, while others looked at me with pity. A few students were standing around the assistant principal in a circle, still pleading their cases that I was a good teacher, and very nice, and that the other students were the problem. He was barely listening as he gently pushed them out the door. When all the kids were gone and the door closed behind them, he looked at me with a little smirk and said, "Yeah, some of them really hate you!"

"I don't know why, honestly," I said. "I'm a very fair and easygoing teacher. I don't usually have issues like this."

"One of them kept saying that you refuse to help him," he said. I immediately responded, "That is not true at all! I ask him multiple times per class if he needs help, and he always says no."

"Another girl said that you said she could choose any book to write her paper about, and you told her that her book choice was bad, and it hurt her feelings."

"I told them that they could choose any book that was an *appropriate* level and subject matter for them and that they should clear their choice with me. She took a Dr. Seuss book and slammed it on the table in front of me. When I said it was definitely not at the right level, she yelled and cursed at me!"

"Well, I think they were just unclear about expectations."

"What!" I said, incredulous. "I explained several times, and it was written on the assignment! I also had the librarian go over how to pick an appropriate book." Why was I having to defend myself against these insane accusations from a bunch of 14-year-olds?

"Well some of them have attention issues. You have to be more patient. I have to go now."

"Wait!" I called out. "Please don't leave yet. I am very confused about where I stand with this class. It seems to me that they were validated in their behavior, and how will I get them to listen to me now?"

"I have a meeting. I can't stay here. Just reestablish expectations tomorrow. Pretend like it's the first day," he said as he walked towards the door.

"Do you have time to meet after school?" I asked desperately. "No, I have another meeting," he responded with mild irritation. "You'll be fine." And with that, he was gone.

I sat and thought about this for a while, and I just couldn't imagine being in that class after they were allowed to talk about me like that. I needed more information from him about how the discussion ended. I emailed him and asked if he had any free time the next day to meet with me and strategize about the class. A while later he responded with, "I am completely booked tomorrow but I've forwarded your email to the chair of your department and the rest of administration. I'm sure one of them would be happy to help you with your classroom management problem."

After that came emails from every administrator saying that they needed more details about the situation. The chair of the department popped her head in not long after and asked me to explain the situation. I did, and she said that I needed to greet each and every student by name at the door, every day. I needed to "teach bell to bell with absolutely no downtime," and the students needed a timed and graded warmup every day. "I understand that the students need structure. And I can assure you that I am giving them that. They are working on a writing assignment (that was mandated by the department), so I am not necessarily *teaching* bell to bell. But I am on my feet, helping them, every second of the class."

"I will be coming by to observe, and the other assistant principal will be observing every day for the next two weeks."

And that was that. It was all my fault, and now I was going to be monitored. Then came the next class, where I broke down and cried uncontrollably. And then the phone call to my husband that I was done.

But here's the thing: The next day, the class I had broken down in front of threw me a party. There were balloons, several cakes that were my favorite flavors (they had asked around), many bunches of flowers, and a lot of stuffed animals (dogs, to be exact — anyone who knows me knows how much I love dogs). More importantly, they had all written me a card about how much they appreciate me, how wonderful I am, and that I just cannot quit because they need kind teachers like me. A lot of them had written individual cards, too. The most surprising part is that the most heartfelt cards came from the students who never seemed to be paying attention.

This was really something. A bunch of 15-year-olds got together to show concern and appreciation for their teacher, who they didn't even really know that well. It was absolutely amazing.

And that's the thing about teaching. It will break you down, tear you apart, and make you feel like you desperately need to get out, but then something wonderful will happen, and it draws you right back in.

I know my books are mostly full of the bad stuff. There is a reason I call it *Teacher Misery*. It's my place to vent. But when I started to collect stories from other teachers and decided to call it *What It's Really Like,* I realized that I needed to include some of the good stuff too. Because if you want to know what it's really like to be a teacher in 2020, it's arduous, impossible, frustrating, and miserable, but it's also heartwarming, fabulous, and *fun*. In this book you'll find a bit of everything, including the usual helicopter parents and awful admin, horrendous student behavior with no consequences, crazy-ass parents and their insane requests; but you'll also find weirdly entertaining stories about a little kid with a foot fetish, a group of teachers chasing a naked kid around the school parking lot, and two pregnant sisters fighting over the same baby daddy in the hallway. There's plenty of gross stuff, like all the strange places kids put their poop and dirty maxi pads, a Barbie in a butthole, and kids who masturbate in class and hump desks. I've also included a sprinkling of tales that will break your heart and a few that will give you the warm and fuzzies we all need to keep going. This book is entertaining, shocking, heartwarming, sad, gross, and sometimes inspiring because *that* is what teaching is really like.

1

A SIMPLE REQUEST

ANONYMOUS

Toward the end of my student teaching experience, a new seventh-grade boy joined my class. I had him sit in an empty seat next to a girl, and on his second day in class, the girl came to me and asked to move seats, saying he was making weird comments and making her feel uncomfortable. I told her to just try to be understanding. The next day, as we were watching a movie, I allowed the kids to have free seating, and I noticed there were empty desks surrounding the new kid. I went and sat by him and asked him how things were going. He got a very earnest look on his face and asked me if he could speak to me in the hall.

Thinking he would tell me about some bullying experience and that I could be his teacher-hero (*fucking novice*), I invited him into the hall. He looked down toward my feet, seeming very uncomfortable.

Me: "What's going on, buddy? Is someone bothering you?"

Boy: "No, it's just... this may be kind of a strange thing to talk about."

Me: "You can talk to me. I'm here for you."

Boy: "I was just wondering if I could smell your feet."

Me: "Umm *no*, that would make me really uncomfortable."

Boy: "I won't tell anyone. No one else would even know."

Me: "I am not okay with that at all.

Boy: "You could just give me one of your shoes for a minute."

Me: "Please go back inside."

I immediately told the counselor, who let out the loudest guffaw I've ever heard. She had me retell the encounter to several others, including the male principal. They contacted the kid's previous school, and it turns out he'd been transferred from the K-8 after asking a young girl if he could smell *her* feet. He eventually got the help he needed, and he ended up thanking me later. But that was the first of many times I questioned my decision to become a teacher.

2

SHIT STUDENTS SAY

J. MORRIS

MAYBE IT SEEMS MEAN TO LAUGH AT DUMB THINGS that students say. If so, please stop reading this book. It ain't for you. For everyone else, enjoy these quotes straight from our future leaders of the world. Keep in mind these are mostly from high school students.

Student: "Why do people wear all black to a funeral?"
Teacher: "It's what you wear when in mourning."
Student: "But what if the funeral is at night?"

"You don't need to breathe when you are sleeping."
"What's on the other side of the world? The map only shows one side. So what's on the other side?"
"If Japan is 14 hours ahead of us, why didn't they warn us about 9/11?"
"Almonds don't have nipples, so how do they make almond milk?"
"How do you spell ADHD?"
"My twin and I don't look alike because I came from the sperm, and she came from the egg."

"This water is so wet."

"I'm known for my self-*defecating* humor."

"This article is hard. How is an obese person supposed to understand it?"

"If coconuts have milk, that means they are mammals."

"Why is the Statue of Liberty holding an ice cream cone?"

"How do I know if that is a capital O or a capital zero?"

"When movies and pictures were only in black and white, did people only see in black and white too?"

"You can't push a cart in the supermarket unless you have a license."

Student has her hand in brownie batter, moving it in circles.
Teacher: "Why do you have your hand in the batter like that?"
Student: "The instructions say mix by hand!"

"Is a digital footprint when you step on your iPad?"

"Why do we pledge to the Republicans every morning?"

"Could you swim under the United States if you had a big enough oxygen tank?"

"Does it rain over the Specific Ocean?"

During a presentation about a local community college, a senior asked, "What kind of rides do you have there?"

Student 1: "Komodo dragons can eat a goat whole."
Student 2: "What's a goat hole? Like its butthole?"

"I know this formula like the back of my head!"

Student: "Why is he always so rude to everyone?"
Teacher: "Don't take it personally. He was born with a chip on his shoulder."

Student: "So, is it, like, implanted under the skin?"
Teacher: "Huh?"
Student: "Is the chip that's on his shoulder implanted under his skin?"

Seventh grader is petting his friend's forehead.
Student (*loud and proud*): "He likes it when I rub his foreskin."
Teacher: "That is his fore*head*, and please keep your hands to yourself and continue your work."
Student: "It's his *skin* on his *forehead*, so it's his *foreskin*! And he likes it when I rub it!"

"Can I go pee? My uterus is full."

Teacher: "Why didn't you complete the worksheet?"
Student: "I didn't know how to do it."
Teacher: "Did you read the directions?"
Student: "There aren't any."
Teacher: "They're right at the top of the page."
Student: "Oh I thought that was a commercial."

High schooler reading *The Diary of Anne Frank* says, "Miss, was this written by Eminem?"
"I can't get pregnant because I only have sex standing up."
"One of the biggest battles of the Civil War was WW2."
"Are dust bunnies real bunnies?"
"All we need to know about sex ed. is that you have to wear two condoms."

Student 1: "Amsterdam? Isn't that the capital of Africa?"
Student 2: "No, stupid. A is the capital of Africa."

Students are learning about female anatomy
Student 1: "Wait. So girls don't pee from their vagina?"
Student 2: "No. They pee from their vagina butthole."

"If pollen is like sperm, can it get me pregnant?"
"When was the war of 1812?"

Student 1: "What's a synonym?"
Student 2: "That's the shit I put on my toast."

Teacher: "During medieval times, some cities would put severed heads on stakes on top of the wall."
Student: "Probably so they could see what was going on on the other side of the wall!"

"Are your twins identical or turtle?"

At a field trip to the aquarium
Student: "Miss! I had my face right up against the octopus tank. I loved it because the octopus pressed his *testicles* right up against the glass near my face!"

Student 1: "What's the capital of New York?"
Student 2: "It's a big apple!"
Student 1: "What do you mean?"
Student 2: "It's just like a big, giant apple!"

Student 1: "Can you get pregnant if you have sex while you're already pregnant?"
Student 2: "Duh! Where do you think twins come from?"

Student: "Hey Jessica! Is your mom still a virgin?"

Student: "Miss, you should watch Game of Thrones because you learn so much about history!"

Teacher: "Our new student just transferred here from Lebanon."
Student: "Does he speak lesbian?"

Student: "Is the ocean salty because it's filled with whale jizz?"

3

AN EMAIL FROM YOUR STUDENT, COOKIE MONSTER

From: Your Student (Cookie Monster?)
To: Teacher
Subject: me confused

Helo, ms,
You have confuse me more
Me thought grade can not go below grade from
before
Me thought assignment optional
Me surprise when grade go down
Me confused on future of grading.

4

POPSICLE DISSERVICE

ANONYMOUS

WHILE TEACHING KINDERGARTEN, DURING MY SCHOOL'S first year of PBIS implementation[1], the class had "earned" a whole-class reward, as stipulated by the PBIS system and had voted to have a Popsicle party. I went out and, of course, spent my own money on these popsicles. On the day of the party, a few students had been having a really rough time making "good choices," so I told those students that I would be picking what color Popsicle they got.

One student, in particular, went home and told his dad that I didn't let him pick his own Popsicle. His dad then sent me a passive-aggressive email saying he was *sure* this couldn't be true. I responded by telling him it was indeed accurate and was a consequence for his son hitting other kids. I also explained that his child still seemed to have a great time eating the red Popsicle I gave him and dancing around to KidzBop.

The next day, an administrator stopped me to ask what had happened. Apparently, the dad had been so upset about the huge Popsicle disservice I had done to his son that he came into the office that day *specifically* to talk to my administrators about it. I explained my reasoning, and once again reiterated that all of the students still received the reward. Admin proceeded to tell me that I shouldn't have chosen the colors for those students because it "wasn't in the spirit of PBIS." But apparently, it was cool that the student had sucker-punched two other kids in my class that day and stabbed one in the hand with a pencil – with zero remorse or consequences.

5

TRASH TALK

From: Vice Principal
To: All Female Employees
Subject: Urgent Bathroom Information!

LADIES,

Let's trash talk for a minute! I had the trash can from a locked staff bathroom removed this morning. No staff bathroom should even have a trash can as we do not even have paper towels. Personal products go into the little silver box next to your keister when you are sitting. Before placing your personal used items in the box, please wrap products that, to put it delicately, need concealing. Twice one direction, 90 degree turn, twice the other direction, so there can be no peeking!

They do not get flushed down the toilet for

this causes great jams! Be thankful you are not a plumber as they shared the quantity of feminine products removed from one of our sewer systems- 60 including 3 maxi pads!

I will refrain from describing in detail what was in the trash can. I was properly schooled by my mother on the disposal of feminine products as we lived up north and had a septic system and it was part of that special talk you get when you become a young lady.

For those offended, I'm sorry. Please don't share with me that you don't get it any longer or that yours was yanked. I may be envious. I'm 57 and it just isn't fair.

Spoken with love and solidarity!

And now the lyrics to Helen Reddy's "I Am Woman." (Google it if you are too young to know this song.)

I am woman, hear me roar
In numbers too big to ignore
And I know too much to go back an' pretend
'Cause I've heard it all before
And I've been down there on the floor
No one's ever gonna keep me down again
Oh yes, I am wise
But it's wisdom born of pain
Yes, I've paid the price
But look how much I gained
If I have to, I can do anything

I am strong
I am invincible
I am woman
You can bend but never break me
'Cause it only serves to make me
More determined to achieve my final goal
And I come back even stronger
Not a novice any longer
'Cause you've deepened the conviction in my soul
Oh yes, I am wise
But it's wisdom born of pain
Yes, I've paid the price
But look how much I gained
If I have to, I can do anything
I am strong
I am invincible...

THE DISH I LIVED IN

ANONYMOUS

OUR KINDERGARTEN CLASS DOES SHOW AND TELL IN the form of an "All About Me" bag. The kids take the bag home and bring it back with something in it from home that tells us a little bit about them.

It was this sweet little girl's turn for the All About Me bag presentation. She first pulled out a birth announcement for her and her twin brother. I thought, "Wow, what a cute thing." She then pulled out a couple of ultrasound photos of them in utero. My students are five and truly had no idea what was going on. I tried to wrap it up, but she reached into the bag and yelled out, "One more thing!" The next thing I know, she is holding a Petri dish that she and her brother were fertilized in through IVF and says, "This is the dish me and my brother grew up in. When we got big enough, the doctor put us inside of our mom." The other students looked really confused, and then started asking me a lot of questions, which I kept dodging. They thought babies came from plastic Petri dishes from this point on. As you could imagine, there were a lot of concerned parents calling the school that evening.

MOMMY'S LITTLE PLAYBOY

2:53 pm

Hey ████████! I just want to let you know there was an innocent game of truth or dare happening at recess and ██████ was dared to kiss a girl in our class across the playground. The guidance counselors met with both of them separately and it's all good, we just want to let the parents know.

✓ 2:53 pm

I'm very sorry that my son is a ho miss ████

I mean playboy that's probably inappropriate lolololol

IT WASN'T PERFUME

ANONYMOUS

I WAS WORKING AS AN ASSISTANT READING COACH IN AN elementary school. I would rush in and out of classrooms all day, working with a variety of students on their fluency, sight words, etc.

One particular student, who was registered as a first grader, would come to school every single day in outfits that consistently surprised me. This varied from short skirts and low cut tank tops to kitten heels and incredibly formal party dresses. I remember asking myself every day why her mother would send her to school dressed like this but decided to mind my own business.

One day, this particular student came into the classroom wearing a rainbow sequin dress and huge, fluffy slippers. She seemed particularly happy. I asked her what she was so pleased about, and she informed me that she had brought her sister's perfume to school and was excited to use it. I told her she could not use it in the classroom (mostly because I was concerned about how some of our sensory sensitive kids might take to a strong smell.)

She wasn't super happy with me and spent the morning pouting and giving me a hard time. Finally, she threw her hand in the air and asked to use the bathroom.

Now, at the time, we were in a room with a bathroom inside the class. She stomped her way to the back of the room, and that's when I saw it. She was holding a bright pink bottle in her hand. And it hit me. That wasn't perfume. That was *mace*.

Have you ever seen the pretty pink mace that you can clip on your keys? Yeah, that one. My first grader had a can of mace inside a high-level sensory sensitive classroom, and she was about to deploy it in the classroom bathroom.

The next few minutes felt like years. I ran towards the bathroom just in time to get hit with the spray flying around the bathroom. I stopped it before it got wildly out of hand, but I had been maced. By a first grader.

I shouted out to the teacher, "Take the children to the library!"

"Why? It's not library time," she responded.

"It's a *special* library time! *Please* just take them!" I pleaded desperately. "Is everything alright?" she asked. *"Please just get the kids out of the room!"* I screamed.

The teacher, realizing I had locked myself in a bathroom with a first grader, finally followed through, and they left the classroom. I emerged and called the office. We were both coughing and crying. It was a mess.

They called her mother because, of course, this was a weapons charge. The mother appeared, looked the girl up and down and yelled, "What are you wearing!?" It turns out that the kid was sneaking clothes into her backpack each morning, getting off the bus, and changing into her outfit of choice at school.

I started laughing uncontrollably. The whole situation was so insane, I just couldn't stop laughing. As I tried to catch my breath and pull myself together during this meeting, I couldn't help but wonder if teaching was really something I wanted to pursue.

VENTING SESSION

From: Your 7th grade student
Subject: on strike

I AM ON STRIKE BECAUSE PERSONALLY I HATE YOU because of everything that has happened in this class throughout the year from you getting mad at me when im mad but you should know I have problems keeping calm. i do horse around sometimes but all you do is talk and then it just feels like i am doing nothing while you just talk about stuff. But when we do things you make it huge and i feel overwhelmed like when we did that game it made me super angry and i wanted to throw the chair i was sitting on at the wall. You moved my seat but other kids rile me up and make me hyper so im not the only one to blame. i have never liked you to begin with, the first time i met you i knew you were going to be mean. Just remember that you were the worse science teacher ever and you probably will be for everyone else like me.

THE DESK HUMPER IN QUESTION

ANONYMOUS

IN THE MIDDLE OF CLASS, A HIGH SCHOOL STUDENT vigorously humped a desk where a conservative Middle Eastern girl was sitting. He really got into it, with passionate sound effects and everything. I wrote him up, and when we called home his father refused to believe the story and demanded a conference because he said I was a liar.

During the conference, they kept asking me if I was *sure* that it was him. I had to provide three "witnesses" from class who saw this happen to prove that my story was correct. (As if I would make something like this up.) Next, they asked me if I misunderstood what he was doing. Perhaps he was just dancing or scratching an itch. I had to go into detail about his actions to fully prove that they were inappropriate and intentional.

Since graduation, this boy has gotten in trouble with the law for breaking and entering and aggravated assault. If only there was an earlier sign of his penchant for socially unacceptable behavior! (*Sigh.*)

THE WORLD'S SHITTIEST GIFTS

J. MORRIS

As a teacher, I don't expect gifts from admin at all. They are just doing their jobs, and don't owe us anything. However, if they are going to put something in our mailbox during Teacher Appreciation Week or the holidays, I'd rather it not be something condescending and obnoxious. A handwritten note would be nice. But a pen taken from the supply closet with a printed piece of paper that says, "You're an INKcredible teacher!" No thanks. Something about it feels like a slap in the face, especially since they make so much more money than us, and often make our jobs much more difficult than they have to be.

Here are some of the worst gifts teachers have received from their administration, ranked from not so bad to the absolute worst (in my opinion):

Not so bad but still pretty bad

- A box of vinyl examination gloves for the staff to

share (*After COVID 19 hit, this turned out to be a great gift!*)

- Two quarters and a votive candle with no wick (*Just a few more quarters and vending machine, here I come! You can also ball up some of that wax and shove it in your ears during the next professional development session!*)
- Toenail clippers (*I mean... Okay. I do have toenails that need clipping.*)
- Toddler sized soup dish and spoon (*Great for regifting at a baby shower for a coworker you don't like?*)
- A burnt cookie in a Ziploc (*A cookie is a cookie and I'm an animal.*)
- A bottle of water and a diet tea mix (*Free bottle of water!*)
- A tiny bottle of glasses cleaner that the local glasses store gave out for free (*Sure, I can use this... you cheap fuck.*)
- One loaf of bread (*Carbs!*)
- One loaf of bread to share amongst 60 people (*Carbs for everyone!*)
- A ream of paper from the supply closet with a post-it that read, "GRATITUDE is the reason for the season!" (*Yeah, I'm grateful for any supplies I didn't pay for. No, I don't like it when I'm told to be grateful. So this pack is coming home with me!*)
- A pocket pack of tissues (*These double as toilet paper, which is a hot commodity!*)
- One liter of apple juice (*My toddler would be psyched!*)

- "Snowman soup:" a few mini marshmallows in a baggie (*My six-year-old would be psyched!*)
- A pen that says "Be Humble" on it (*A free pen is a free pen. And you can relieve stress by scratching off that obnoxious message.*)
- A single Hershey's Kiss (*I'll never complain about chocolate. But I will complain about you being a cheap piece of shit!*)
- A spatula (*Can I hit someone with it?*)
- A single can of seltzer (*Is it flavored? If so, that's fancy. If not, my grandma would be psyched.*)
- A fortune cookie (*Fun to smash!*)
- Reusable ice cubes (*Great re-gift for someone you don't give a shit about at all!*)
- One highlighter with an index card that said, "You're the highlight of your students' day!" (*Who doesn't love a cheesy-ass pun?*)
- Goats were bought for people in a village in a third world country in honor of the teachers at our school (*While this does absolutely nothing for the teacher, and is a bit strange, at least it is helping people.*)
- One teabag (*Anything involving caffeine is acceptable.*)
- Pizza but strictly limited to ONE SLICE (*Just enough pizza to make us all want more pizza, that we can't have.*)
- A tiny plastic bucket (*Is it for my tears?*)
- A book called "How to Be a Better Catholic" given out for free by the local church (*It's a book, so I won't say it's completely useless. But, really?*)

Completely useless

- Leftover restaurant discount cards from a school fundraiser that were completely expired (*You can use it as a fan when they are still fixing the AC for the 8th year in a row...?*)
- A broken clock (*Maybe they didn't know it was broken? One can hope...*)
- A sheet of bubble wrap that they called "Stress Relief" (*Some people really enjoy this?*)
- A raffle for a pack of hair rubber bands and a hairbrush. A bald guy won. (*He can exchange it at the Dollar Tree for another cheap treasure!*)
- A glow stick with an index card that said, "Thanks for helping our school SHINE!" (*Cool. I'll save it for that rave I'm planning to go to when I get in my time machine later...*)
- An ornament that said, "Merry Christmas 1999," given in the year 2005 (*Christmas was like particularly merry that year though...*)
- A seashell (*Did someone actually get out there on the beach and collect these? That's sort of amusing.*)

What the fuck were they thinking?

- A coupon for a hug from a predatory principal who is way too touchy-feely with the female staff (*Use this to get him fired.*)
- Erotic books written by an admin's wife (*I think this could be grounds for termination for sexual harassment. If your admin gave you a copy of 50 Shades of Gray or a book called "My Ass is*

Haunted by the Gay Unicorn Colonel[1]," I'm *pretty sure you'd have grounds for some kind of lawsuit*.)

- A photo of the school (*I don't like seeing it when I arrive in the morning, why would I want to think about it at any other time?*)
- A box of thank you notes with instructions that read, "Please write these out for your most appreciated students" (*So your gift to me is giving me extra work? This is what the words FUCK and YOU were created for*.)
- A chocolate bar with a customized wrapper with a picture of all administrators on it (*I do enjoy chocolate and I guess after I eat it I can use the wrapper to wipe my ass?*)
- An actual rock with the words "You Rock!" written on it in Sharpie (*Which secretary did you force to sit there and write on rocks all afternoon?*)
- The principal sent out an email that he would buy a round of drinks at the Mexican restaurant next door the night before break. A lot of teachers went and ordered drinks but admin never showed up. They had to pay themselves. (*Total douche move*.)
- A book about classroom management written by the principal (*I'd ask him to come and demonstrate on my worst class, and just sit back and enjoy the show*.)
- A digital copy of a "Work Smarter Not Harder" newsletter written by the Board of Ed. Soon after came an angry email that said too many people were marking the email as spam, and

they should be grateful for it. Admin told us
that the school district spent thousands on
newsletter subscription, and IT was forcibly
unblocking the newsletter emails. For the rest of
the year, the same email address would send a 6
AM wakeup email. (*I'd make a fake email and
start sending back videos of goats yelling.*)

- One box of chocolate for a staff of 200 to share
  (*They can each chew it, spit it out, and pass it on!
  What a bonding experience.*)
- A picture of admin's faces floating in a snow
  globe (*Great stress relief to smash it in the
  parking lot.*)
- A note that we could leave an hour early the
  day before break, but we had to use personal
  time and clock it in (*I can use my personal time
  that I'm contractually entitled to? Thanks, dick.*)
- A cartoon drawing of the principal (*Just think of
  all the weird things you could do with this! Tape
  it to your punching bag or toilet seat! Use it to
  pick up dog crap! The possibilities are endless!*)[2]
- One paper clip shaped like an apple (*You could
  unfold it and use it as a weapon, if needed?*)
- A mandatory invite to a staff luncheon that cost
  $15 per person (*Wait. I have to come to a lunch
  that I have to pay for? COME ON! Do you
  WANT us to hate you?*)

AN UNFORGETTABLE FIRST DAY

WILLIE DASIGNER, CHARLESTON, SOUTH CAROLINA

IT WAS 1994, AND IT WAS MY SECOND YEAR TEACHING at one of the most challenging schools in the district. It was rough. And odd things happened a lot.

It was the first day of school, and in the middle of my very first lesson, a student stood up and said, "Mister!" and then nothing else. I said, "What is it?" but she just stood there. "Mister!" she called out. Again, I asked what she wanted. At that moment, she held her hand to her mouth and started projectile vomiting. This caused the vomit to spray out of both sides of her hands, hitting students on either side of the aisle and landing on their desks. Screaming ensued. Kids began to scatter. And a horrendous, acidic smell began to envelop the room.

I quickly told the student to go to the nurse and stepped aside. She took a step or two, and then vomited onto the floor, which splattered onto a few students' legs and one girl's toes. More scattering and more stink. She went to the middle of the room, turned towards the class and spewed even more vomit out of her mouth. Now headed towards the door, the students nearby scrambling to avoid being hit, she stopped, looked at all of us again, turned the knob and opened the door, but not before vomiting all over the door, including the knob. At this point, everyone was up out of their seats, and the fumes of the vomit were too much to bear. More students started vomiting just from the smell.

I was yelling the whole time for the student to go to the nurse's office, and several kids began to yell at her to leave. She walked out of the door and closed it behind her, as vomit streaked down the back of the door. We were trapped. No one was going to touch that door handle.

Students began to open the bank of windows on the far side of the room while I hit the emergency call button. As more students headed towards the windows, the office chimed in. I asked them to come open the door, and they didn't understand why. They couldn't seem to understand why I wasn't going to stand in the vomit and turn the vomit-covered knob to free my students from the vomit tomb.

While talking to the office on the intercom, I felt a little nauseous myself because the warm spring breeze picked up a little and spread the vomit smell through the room, even stronger than before. I threw up into a trashcan as two students threw up out the window into the alley below.

So there I stood, assessing the classroom. There was vomit all over the desks, the floor, the door, and the kids who were hit with the spew were still in an uproar to get out of the room to clean the now-drying vomit off their skin and clothes. I heard more gagging at the windows. Finally, the custodian opened the door and released us. It was truly an unforgettable first day.

WHAT IS THIS SORCERY?

To: Olaf's mom
Subject: Olaf's HW
Good evening,
I just wanted to inform you that Olaf did not
have his homework again this morning but by
the end of the day, another student's homework
appeared in his backpack. It had the student's
name crossed off and Olaf's was written
on top.

To: Olaf's teacher
From: Olaf's mom
Subject: Re: Olaf's HW
Yes, I have seen it for myself. Things being in
Olaf's bags that he didn't put there and have
had to have him bring it back to school. The
word of God teaches that this is sorcery. God
promises to destroy sorcery and those who
practice it. God's word does not come back

unfulfilled so I am not worried. Also I find it strange that another student's name was on Olaf's work. Let's see what else appears in the next few days. Enjoy your day.

To: Olaf's mom
Subject: Olaf's cellphone
Good evening,
I just wanted to inform you that Olaf had his phone confiscated during a test today. To retrieve it, you will need to come to the main office.

To: Olaf's teacher
From: Olaf's mom
Subject: Re: Olaf's cellphone
You are playing games but God of Israel's words say your mischief shall recoil upon your head and you will fall into your own pit.

14

EVERYONE DESERVES TO FEEL SPECIAL

ANONYMOUS

I HAVE SPENT ROUGHLY 4,000 DAYS OF MY ADULT LIFE in a middle school. They have not all been pleasant, but there have been a few days, like today, when something great happens.

One of my male students kept asking me when the Student Council was going to start selling candy grams for Valentine's Day. For $1, the student can send a few Hershey's kisses to a recipient of their choice, along with a message. This afternoon the same boy requested 60 tags. He had $60 on him. My ears perked up right away because I didn't want an angry email from a parent asking why I allowed him to spend so much money on candy. He assured me that his parents knew and that he had a plan.

It turns out that this boy researched and found the names for every single girl in sixth grade and their homeroom numbers, so he could send them each a candy gram on Valentine's Day. He printed out his own labels with a special message that read, "Everyone deserves to feel special on Valentine's Day," and he did not include his name.

As if this wasn't sweet enough, he used his own money. He gets $5 a week for doing chores, and he saved for three months. There are a lot of crazy kids who make our jobs more difficult, but there are a few exceptional ones who make it all worth it.

A PROBLEM WITH NO SOLUTION

Today 7:28 AM

Good morning. ███████ had trouble this morning putting on his socks and sneakers..I'm gonna leave him home again I will send a letter tmrw

DO NOT EMAIL THAT PICTURE!

ANONYMOUS

THIS IS A STORY FROM MY FIRST YEAR OF TEACHING, about midway through the most challenging year of my life. My school site had a computer monitoring system that allowed me to see the students' screens on my own computer. To keep track of off-task students, I would take a screenshot of their screen, so I had a list of who to talk to later.

One day during a test, one of my eighth-grade girls had a Facebook chat open, so I did my typical screenshot and told her to get back to work. After the class had left, I got around to looking at the screenshot and realized the two had been discussing whether or not they would have sex that day. I thought this was bad enough, but then I noticed there was a collection of pictures to the right of the screen, and right at the bottom was a photo of her boyfriend's penis. I immediately freaked out and thought to delete it, but then I remembered it was my work computer, and I had no clue if the district could access our screenshots or saved pictures. I didn't want to have a screenshot of a penis on my computer without anyone knowing why it was there!

I emailed my vice principal and asked if I should delete it and if I should report it to anyone else. She didn't reply, and I ended up running into her in the hallway during the next period. I told her the issue, and she told me to email her the image, and she'd deal with it. Thinking back, she was quite distracted when giving this direction. I went back to my own room, and because my next class was starting, I began teaching, making a note to send the picture later. Not two minutes after class started, our on-site police officer burst into my room and exclaimed, "Do not email that picture!" He confiscated my computer and the student computer that had been used. It turns out that emailing the picture was incredibly bad advice as this is considered distribution of child pornography. The officer had to take a report, including all of my personal information. They assured me it was just procedure, and I was not in trouble. This didn't ease my mind at all, and I thought I had really messed up. I worried that not only would I lose my job, but I might be arrested.

Since the picture was only of the penis and there was no way to determine who exactly it belonged to, it did not end up being considered a child porn situation. The female student was given a few days of in-school suspension, and the issue was dropped. But I learned a vital lesson: if I ever see nudity on a student's computer, wipe it from my brain and pretend it never happened. And definitely do not take a screenshot!

SO GOOD BUT SO BAD BUT SO GOOD

To: Chemistry teacher
From: Brak's mom
Subject: Lesson on Pot

HELLO,

I was wondering, since Brak is in chemistry, could you do a brief unit on marijuana and the effect on the teenage brain? Brak has been smoking a lot of pot which worries me. I taught school for 42 years and have students smoke too much or move on to other drugs. I lost students who started smoking pot and moved onto LSD. He won't listen to me and has invited me to join him a few times, which I will probably do when he is older. I figure I'm 71 now so why the hell not? I personally think it should be legalized. I tried it once in college and it felt so good I knew it would be bad. In fact, it was great so it scared the shit out of me. Can you talk to Brak about it? Thanks.

SHIT IN THE VENDING MACHINE, ETC.

ANONYMOUS

ON MY FIRST DAY OF TEACHING, I SUGGESTED AN activity that might get kids to read and write more. A colleague yelled, "Shut up!" in front of the entire faculty. I couldn't understand why at the time, but now I know that the school had much more significant issues than motivating students to read.

The school is fucking crazy. Kids shit on the floor and in the hall in front of the office. They shit in vending machines, and instead of getting rid of the machine, they just turned it around. Girls leave used pads in front of class-room doors.

But that's not the craziest shit that takes place. During my first year, a male student said to me, "You need pussy 'cause you so stressed." I wrote him up. When the dean read the referral, he had to put his head down on his desk as he was laughing so hard. The dean gave the kid cake because it was his birthday.

A few years back, I broke up a fight in my class. The principal called Child Protective Services on me because I touched the students as I broke them apart. That same year, another fight broke out in my classroom. I did nothing. Why would I want Protective Services called on me again? The same principal called Protective Services because I did nothing and "endangered the students by not intervening."

Recently, at a faculty meeting, a brand new teacher suggested that we all do "walk-throughs" of our colleagues' classrooms to ensure we are all using "equitable practices." I didn't hesitate before yelling, "Shut up!" with glee.

IT'S CALLED LIFE

To: Barnabas' mom
From: Barnabas' teacher
Subject: Lunch detention

Good afternoon,
This message is to inform you that Barnabas
will be serving lunch detention tomorrow due to
excessive tardies. If you have any question
please let me know.

To: Barnabas' teacher
From: Barnabas' mom
Subject: Re: Lunch detention

It's called life. I'm "tardy" every day to work
and other events with no reprimand. His father
and I talked about it. At this point we don't
know whether to be annoyed with you and the

school and the constant issues you have with our son or what. He said it's difficult to get from class to class without running. Whew! I can't wait for this year to be over!

SHIT SHOW

CHRISTINA, NEW YORK CITY

I took a job teaching kindergarten at a renewal school (a failing school that is supposed to be getting extra resources) in NYC. We had almost no resources and definitely no support from administration.

One kid was having a rough first day, feeling anxious and such. At one point, he went into the bathroom, which was in the classroom. After a few minutes, I had to knock on the door to check on him. As he quietly opened the door, I could see the sadness, fear, and anxiety in his face. And then I looked up. He had explosive diarrhea that was *everywhere*. I mean, it was up the walls, all over the toilet and the floor, and all over him. I was alone and needed to take the class to the cafeteria for lunch, so I called the office for some assistance. They told me to take him to the nurse. The poor kid had to walk down the hall with the rest of the class to the cafeteria, and then the nurse's office. When we got there, the nurse turned us away and told me that she couldn't do anything about it. She said I should take him back to class and call his parents! Since I didn't have a phone in my room, I had to walk with him to the main office to call his mom. All while this kid had shit dripping down his body.

I wasn't allowed to change him or touch him, so we walked back to class, and I had him sit on a stool while we waited for his mom. After he was gone, I had to clean up the poop that was on the stool and tracked onto the floor. It was a shit show... literally!

SUPPORTIVE STRANGER

> Hello! This is Mrs. P▊▊▊
> I'm P▊▊▊'s social studies
> teacher. He has had an incredi-
> bly difficult time in class today.
> He refuses to meet any class-
> room expectations. He has his
> sweatshirt on his head, refuses
> to remove it, refusing to move
> seats, and has been very rude
> to his peers and myself.

Oct 26, 11:19 AM

B Wrong number but whoop his ass

▊▊▊ • 12:20 AM

22

SHAME

ANONYMOUS

I HAD ONLY BEEN TEACHING FOR THREE YEARS. IT WAS my first year at a new elementary school, and I quickly learned it was completely run by the parents. I heard so many horror stories of parents bitching and admin bending to their will immediately. I tried to fly under the radar as much as possible.

I had a student in one of my classes who I'll call "Rufus." Rufus was actually my favorite student. He was bright, creative, hilarious, and very sweet when he wanted to be. He also had some concerning behavior problems. He would shout insults at other students across the room, kick other students, throw things, scream, slam chairs on the ground, etc. I have a soft spot for kids like that. I did everything I could to keep him calm, happy, and in the classroom. He refused to do work most of the time, but if he was relatively quiet and nonviolent, I considered it a good day. His mother was very supportive of me at first, even going so far as to warn me that another mom was talking shit about me in their fifth-grade Mommy Facebook Group. She had sent e-mails to me thanking me profusely for working with her son. So even though he had some behavior issues to work on, I thought I had his parents' support.

One day the kids were taking a test. During a test students are not allowed to talk or cause any sort of distraction. Rufus had finished his test quickly and began talking to himself, loudly. I reminded him that talking is not allowed during a test. He was quiet for a minute, but then started talking again. I went over to his desk and told him that if he spoke again, I would ask him to move out into the hallway so that everyone could finish their test. He was quiet for a moment but then started talking again. I asked him to go into the hall so as not to distract the others. He got up and yelled, "I think you have autism!" at me, and left in a huff. I filled out the standard referral form for disrespect, and when everyone was gone I called his parents. Neither one picked up, so I wrote an email explaining what had happened and expressing my hope that we could work together to help Rufus with self-control. His mom responded by saying, "WOW! Shame on you! Your behavior is unacceptable! You, as a new teacher, should be ASHAMED! I will speak with my lawyer and make an appointment with your supervisors from there."

I was very upset because I had been bending over backward to help this kid. He was the one I spent the most effort on out of all 45 of my students. I loved this kid. And now his mom decided that I was enemy #1, and I didn't really understand why.

She did call my supervisors. She went all the way up to the district level to complain about me, telling people that I was cursing at the kids, that I picked favorites, that I singled her child out and decided to "make life a living hell for him." A meeting was held with both parents and before the meeting, the guidance counselor told me we need to just "let mom unload and not say much." I was not excited about being a punching bag, but isn't that what being a teacher today is all about?

She and her husband came in with a written list of grievances that she angrily spewed at me. She accused me of targeting her son and getting him into trouble for nothing. She said that he has never had so many issues, and therefore it must be my fault. The dean interjected and told her that actually, he has been to the dean's office half as many times as he had last year and that his behavior problems began the first week of kindergarten. The principal didn't bother to attend the meeting, but she had told me that I was actually being too lenient with him, which I shared. At the end of the meeting, Rufus' mom told us that she could never do the work that we do, that she has so much respect for teachers, etc. But she never apologized.

We had a series of meetings following that because his parents were convinced that he was either gifted or needed special education. Mom once again threatened the school as a whole for neglecting her child by not outright offering him a specialized education plan before he was even tested. We explained that the process can either be initiated by the parents or by the teachers, whenever deemed necessary and that if they believed Rufus needed a special plan, they were welcome to start the paperwork. (In my opinion, Rufus was capable of excellent work, when he bothered to do it. But usually, he simply refused.) By the end of the year, he had a specialized education plan that included things like allowing him to carry toys in his pockets to play with in class at any time, unlimited bathroom breaks, 50% more time on all assessments, etc.

By April, I already knew I wanted to quit this school. I interviewed and was offered a job teaching at another school, so I began counting down the days at this one. Sometime in May I was called into the principal's office for my year-end evaluation. My principal told me that although I am a good teacher, and she is impressed with what I have going on in my classroom, I would not be asked back next year because Rufus' mom had spread so many rumors that my "reputation at this school will never recover." She offered to "allow" me to resign rather than face non-renewal. I resigned. And I called the other school where I had been offered a job and turned it down.

On the second to last day of school I received a handwritten note from yet another mom, this time accusing me of child abuse. Her daughter had to walk laps at recess the previous day because she was not following directions in class. This was a grade-wide policy. We had recess at 1 PM, where she walked her laps while wearing a sweatshirt and refusing to drink water. I had her in class from 1:30-4. She was completely fine. Apparently she went home, cried all night, and complained about pain in her legs until her mom wrote this letter. I couldn't help but laugh out loud when I read it. Two more days and this shit would no longer be my problem.

On the last day of school, I ran into my principal on my way out. She asked me if I had found a job yet. I told her no, but there were many opportunities on the horizon. She looked at me with so much pity I wanted to punch her. I left and sang my heart out all the way home. I will never teach again.

23

MAYBE WE GO TO THE SAME THERAPIST!

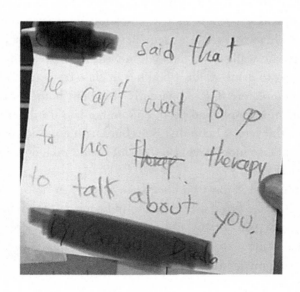

24

HOW TO GET FREE TUTORING

ANONYMOUS, LOS ANGELES, CALIFORNIA

I was teaching seventh graders at a Catholic School. It was only my second year. It was 2:45 PM on a Friday, and I was reading to the class. It started to smell like something was burning. I looked up from my book and saw a haze in the room. A kid who was sitting about three feet from me had lit the motherfucking carpet on fire!

I walked over there, stomped on it, and shouted at the top of my lungs, "Did you just light a fire in our classroom!?" He barely looked up and said, "Well, I didn't mean to burn a hole in the carpet. I just wanted to see if I could light my shoes on fire."

It turns out that he brought matches to school and spent most of the day trying to light other students' arm hairs on fire. We had a closet area where apparently he had been setting various objects on fire, I found out later. I walked him to the principal, just two doors down from me, returned to class, and continued yelling at the class for not telling me the kid was lighting things on fire all day. I still don't know how I didn't see or hear it myself.

The boy got suspended, but the principal called me in to ask if I would teach him after school while he was suspended, for free of course. When I declined, he asked if I could give *him* lessons so he could tutor the kid himself, which he did.

25

A NEW PERSPECTIVE

class. These behaviors are starting to impede his classmates' ability to learn and it's becoming increasingly difficult to teach without having to stop and wait for him to stop yelling across the room.

He has been given multiple warnings in class and numerous opportunities to correct this behavior. I would hate to see this begin to affect his grade or his classmates' grades. He is a very bright young man and I really do enjoy teaching him. I just want to be transparent about the issue and I want him to see that we are a team and our number one priority is his academic success.

Thank You.

J
to me
3 hours ago Details

Maybe you are a boring teacher.

26

I'LL ALWAYS WONDER

ANONYMOUS

I STARTED OFF MY HIGH SCHOOL TEACHING CAREER AS A long term sub, midway through the school year. Luckily, at the end of the year, I found out that a teacher was moving, so a position opened up, and I applied and got the job. Once I was given my roster, I was really pleased to see that there were several students from the classes that I had subbed for. I felt that I had developed a good rapport with my past students and was looking forward to continuing those relationships. After the school year started, I was slapped with the difficult reality of acclimating to the politics of the school and navigating the numerous student issues. I felt confident enough in reaching out to counselors when I was concerned, especially about students I knew from my subbing experience.

One of those students was a young man who was excited about learning and demonstrated an innate skill for the material. He came to class excited to learn and seemed pleased to have me as his teacher once again. As the year progressed, I noticed that his mood was erratic, and his work ethic and performance had drastically worsened. I emailed his counselor three times but never heard back. Being a new teacher, I hadn't yet gained the confidence to call home with what seemed like unfounded concerns at the time.

On the last day of school, I noticed that the same student seemed agitated and stressed out. I attributed his emotional state to finals week and assured him he would be fine once finals were over. At our last staff meeting of the year, we were told that a murder had occurred and that it involved some of our students. I fervently hoped that my name would not be called as a teacher of any students involved, but my hopes came crashing down when they called my name to stay after the meeting. When they told me that my student, the one I had been concerned about, was involved, I felt like reality suspended itself. In what world was the kind, mature, smart young man that I knew somehow caught up in such a monstrous crime? Amidst the ensuing rumors and whispered conversations between staff members about "those" students and how they just knew something was off, I struggled to understand and recognize the feelings around the school.

I reached out to the young man's father as a way to soothe my own guilt in feeling that I had not done enough to stop him from going down this road. He asked if I would attend the arraignment and be a character witness. I attended the arraignment, full of doubts about my position as a teacher. Aren't we supposed to be there for our students when they need it the most? Was this crime reflective of his true nature? I didn't think so. I felt almost guilty sitting in the gallery, along with the parents of the boy who had died and could not reconcile my being there. After speaking with the principal, it was clear to me that taking any part in the trial or following proceedings would put me squarely on one side of the case, and this side would not necessarily be the best decision for my career. I told his father that I would not be able to take part any longer and tried to move on.

I didn't follow the case that summer because I couldn't stand the sadness or the guilt I felt. Last summer, I received a handwritten letter from this student left in my school mailbox by his cousin. He is still in prison and will be for the next 50 years. He praised me for being a teacher who cared and expressed his gratitude that I came to his arraignment, a fact he didn't learn until years later. He also had somehow found out that I was pregnant and congratulated me, saying that I would be a terrific mother. This letter still makes me cry, bringing back the guilt and yet with it, the affirmation that I did something right by caring for my students. In that letter, I see the convicted felon with his significant life mistakes, and I also see the 17-year-old boy showing the class his amazing drawings and excitedly taking part in class activities. I'll always wonder if I could have intervened more and perhaps even have prevented this somehow.

This experience taught me a lot about teaching. The right answers are sometimes hard to find, and every kid teaches us something about life.

ALL IS FORGIVEN

you are the
best tutor teacher
I have had. I
will miss you load.
Sorry for when I
used to be a
cunt and walk
out love

NOT A PRIORITY

ANONYMOUS

I TEACH THIRD GRADE, SO KEEP IN MIND THAT THEY ARE eight years old while you read this shit.

I was the lucky winner to be chosen to teach the kid with the worst behavior problems in the school. I work in a Title 1 school, and 97% of the kids are on free and reduced lunch. Many are living in situations with daily abuse and horrible living conditions. Behavioral issues are prevalent, but this boy was honestly the worst of the worst.

The entire year this boy camped out underneath my desk. He had his own desk, right in front, just as his individualized ed. plan had stated. But he refused to sit in a desk from the first day of school. I am pretty chill with accommodating kids and didn't mind him sitting on the floor. He didn't move from under my desk all year and he refused to do any work. No one could make him do anything, including administration. He literally watched YouTube music videos all day in my class with headphones in. He would get physically violent when I would try to force him to do any work. Mind you, the work I would give him was quite easy. I would even write words in highlighter and try to have him trace over it. He would do one word and flip the fuck out. He would throw everything off my desk and try to flip it over. He threw books and staplers across the room, spit in my face, and nothing was done, *ever*. Finally, admin agreed to come and "evaluate" him to get him help. They crouched down underneath a desk with a clipboard and pencil and tried to get him to do work. They tried begging him and offering him rewards the entire time, as I had done in the early months. I almost gave the kid a high five because he took their work and tore it into tiny little pieces, and one by one rolled the paper into spitballs and spit it at a district administrator's face. Their only response was to criticize everything I tried during their one classroom observation. I was seven months pregnant by this time, so I didn't give a fuck what he did anymore, and I was afraid for my safety. I stopped worrying about him and let him sit and watch YouTube.

He repeatedly got into physical fights with adults and even cornered my principal and kicked and punched her. He grabbed a tennis racket and threatened to beat her with it. The district still refused to move him into a different classroom environment. My absolute last straw before I went on maternity leave was the fact that he brought a knife to school and only got suspended for three days. It was only found because it fell out of his pocket. After the incident, he told me, "My other person does things, and I know they are wrong, but I can't stop him from doing bad things."

He was in my class until the last day of school. Clearly, he had an emotional disability and needs medication and help. His mom would try to fill out the paperwork to get him evaluated, but I found out she couldn't even read most of the questions she was given.

My school had gotten an eight million dollar grant from

the government around the same time, but I couldn't even get an aide to help me when he had to be put in full body holds. I fought so hard to get him help and to protect myself and my 29 other students, but at the end of the day, he just wasn't a priority for them.

29

I'M AFRAID THAT'S YOUR JOB!

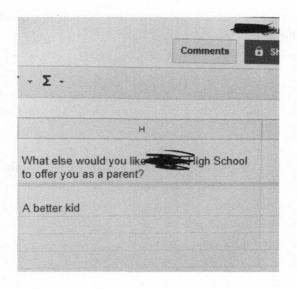

30

YOU MADE IT! BUT...

ANONYMOUS

Here is a brief summary of my first year of teaching:

September: I welcome what I was told was "the worst kindergarten class the school has ever seen" into first grade.

October: One girl screams all day. *Every day*. Another girl demands to go home, and when I tell her that is not possible, she pees her pants and splashes around in her puddle of pee on the floor. She then feels the need to dip her hands in the puddle and wipe it on her face.

November: My classroom is set on fire while being used for an after school program. The cause of the fire would not be told to the teachers; however, when questioned by the fire marshal, they said it was most definitely *not* an electrical fire. Everything in our room is ruined. Two days later, my aide collapses in the stairwell. I call 911. He passes away.

December: Our class is now called "the worst first-grade class the school has ever seen." The same girl still screams all day. Kids are starting to beat the shit out of each other.

January: One of my students stabs me in the face with a pencil because she doesn't want to do writing, and I was trying to help her.

February: Our new aide quits the day before break. He doesn't even tell me. He just never shows up again.

March: We are finally told we *might* be able to move back into our room because the repairs from the fire are almost done. When we ask about furniture and supplies, the administration tells us that there is nothing left in the budget for furniture. This conversation takes place following the principal showing off all of the new furniture in his office.

April: The month seems to be ending without a terrible incident, but on April 30th, I pull a bedbug off of a kid. Unfortunately, knowing the protocol, I have to put it in a plastic bag and hand-deliver it to administration. When I show them what I found, they tell me that I can't call it a bedbug because I am not an expert and cannot officially make that call. They say they can't do anything until I catch at least four more.

May: We all barely survive each other. I try to summon the strength to get through just one more month with my class.

June: The principal calls me in for a meeting and tells me that I will be looping to second grade with the same kids I had that year. *Fuck. My. Life.*

PLEASE EXTEND MY WARMEST CONGRATULATIONS

To: Bathsheba's teacher
From: Bathsheba's mom
Subject: Last night's reading

Hello. I am sorry that Bathsheba did not complete last night's reading assignment. Her stuffed animals were having a wedding.

AN INTRO TO PUBLIC SCHOOL

JAY, NEW JERSEY

I SWITCHED FROM TEACHING PRIVATE SCHOOL TO public school 15 years ago. I thought, "Kids are kids. How different could they be?" I couldn't have been more wrong.

It was the morning of my first day at my new school. I was sitting in the faculty room, drinking my first cup of coffee, when a teacher ran in and yelled that there was a fight. Another teacher and I ran out into the hall and into the middle of a particularly vicious fight between two pregnant girls. We jumped in and separated them as best we could. Eventually, a vice principal showed up and took them away. It turns out they were beating each other up because they were pregnant by the same guy. And also, *they were sisters.*

I went back into the faculty room and gulped the rest of my now cold coffee. I called my wife and asked if she thought the Catholic school would give me my job back.

COMPLETELY UNDERSTANDABLE

Dear Mr. Boyle,

I am sorry ████ did not finish his math in class yesterday. It seems he was distracted by Michael Jackson songs in his head. Please let me know if this continues to be a problem.

A concerned parent.

PET CEMETERY IN MY LOCKER

ANONMOUS

A FEW YEARS AGO, I HAD A VERY "INTERESTING" student who came across a dead cat as she walked to school. She, of course, felt bad for the cat, so she proceeded to pick it up and bring it to school with her. Another student reported that they watched her put the dead cat into her locker (mind you this is a junior in high school) and that it smelled horrible. Eventually, she was brought in and asked about why she had put a dead cat in her locker. She told our assistant principal that she was "going to bring the cat back to life with her powers." She was suspended for a week, and her powers couldn't undo that.

35

KEEP IT FRESH

Grades Inbox ☆

to me
May 13 Details

Yo wat up my homie. I was jus wonderin about dat
persuasive advertizement. I did it and turned it in. Honesly,
even if i get 1 point it much better than a zero.
Keep it Fresh.

****Sent from via Google Apps****

A BRIEF INTERRUPTION

COLIN T., NORTH CAROLINA

IT WAS THE FIRST MONTH OF MY FIRST YEAR OF teaching. Admin had been telling us for weeks how important it was to have students take the district tests seriously. It would reflect poorly on our school if they didn't do well and could lose us funding. During the first test it took 30 minutes just to get them all logged on to the computers. Once they were all finally quiet and had just begun working, there was a knock on my door. I opened it and saw my principal, four police officers, and a German shepherd.

The principal explained that they were doing a "random" drug sweep. I told him that we had just started testing, and I was worried it might interfere. He assured me that it was fine and would only take a moment.

The students shuffled into the hallway, and the dog went in. About two minutes later, one of the policemen stuck his head out and waved us over. We both thought they had found something. Nope. The dog got excited and shit all over the floor. And it wasn't just one pile of poop. There were little piles of diarrhea all over the room. The smell was unbearable, and my classroom had no windows.

The janitor was called down, and he didn't even blink. He just started wiping the shit up. The kids had been in the hallway for about 20 minutes and knew exactly what had happened. Some thought it was hilarious, while others were worried about the test.

We eventually went back in, but it still smelled like shit, and there was an added bleach odor too. The kids went wild, and the principal told me he wouldn't blame me if I did nothing with them for the rest of the day, even though they had been logged in to this timed test for over an hour already.

37

CAN'T GET NUTTIN PAST HER!

BOYS PEE OUTSIDE

CHELSEA, CALIFORNIA

To set up the scene, I taught in a Title 1 elementary school where the student population was 95% English Language Learners. Halfway through the school year, I got asked to take over my coworker's class because she was on medical leave for an insane injury that was caused by a kindergartener. They didn't want another substitute coming into the class, so they pulled me to continue with the students for the rest of the year.

Her class had recently acquired a new student I'll call Luigi, and I could tell he was already going to be an issue. This was a kindergarten class, so the students would get picked up from the classroom by parents, or older brothers and sisters. Pick-up time is always a crazy mess trying to make sure the classroom is cleaned up, and each student goes to the right place. Luigi's brother came to pick him up, and when I called his name, Luigi was nowhere to be found. Once all my other students were gone, I began to frantically walk around the school, still looking for the student. My coworker, who was familiar with this student's antics, said she would start searching for him outside of the school grounds.

Ten minutes went by, and I got a call from my coworker saying she had found Luigi two blocks away, peeing on a house! I couldn't believe what I was hearing. I alerted the office and told them to please call the student's guardian.

A half-hour went by, and Luigi's mom did not come to pick him up, but rather his extremely intoxicated uncle came banging into the office, blaming me for his nephew escaping, yelling at the secretary, and grabbing the student. We alerted authorities that the student left with a drunk man.

The next day the student arrived at school with a hand-written note from his mom. The note said that I was irresponsible and that I hadn't let her son use the restroom, so he did what he had to do. The note literally said, "He is a boy and boys pee outside." It didn't seem to matter to her that he had escaped school, jumped a fence, walked two blocks down a busy road, and peed on a house.

ONE BARBIE SHORT

BROOKE FULLER, MERCED, CALIFORNIA

IN MY FIRST YEAR OF TEACHING KINDERGARTEN, I HAD a really naughty student. She was constantly doing bizarre things in class and on the playground. One day, she got in trouble for something and was sitting at a lone desk while the other students were getting to choose a free-play activity in the classroom.

I have a playhouse in my room that has kitchen tools and, of course, dolls and Barbies. While playing, a student came up to me to tell me that the naughty student had taken a doll. I looked at the student, and she was still sitting at her desk and didn't appear to have a doll. I looked at my student, frustrated, and said, "She doesn't have a doll. She's in trouble! Where would she put the doll anyway?" My student looked me dead in the eye and said, "It's in her butt."

After asking her several times if she was sure, I asked the student if she had a doll, and she said no. I asked her to get out of her chair and she proceeded to stand up and walk with a crazy limp because she was trying to hide the Barbie that was in her butt. The playhouse is one Barbie short now.

PAYMENT REQUEST FROM FORMER STUDENT

42

MAGIC WAND

ANONYMOUS

I WAS TEACHING KINDERGARTEN AND ONCE A WEEK WE had a "show and tell" session. We were studying fairy tales, and one of my students was overly excited to share what she brought with her that day. As we were thinking about descriptive words and vocabulary, she began her share moment, explaining that she brought a big, sparkly, pink magic wand with her!

She pulled a giant pink "adult toy" from her bag and began to explain that she found it in her mom's room. She attempted to show the class how it lights up and moves. I scrambled to move her along and said that her object was fantastic, but let's put it away and let someone else have a go!

It was the most awkward conversation I had to have with a parent. And yes, I had to touch it to put it away.

HAPPY TO BE OF SERVICE

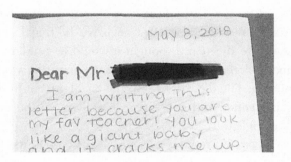

44

HEY! TEACHER! LEAVE THOSE FROGS ALONE!

KRISTIN C., MARIN COUNTY, CALIFORNIA

I'M A MIDDLE SCHOOL SCIENCE TEACHER, AND WHEN I first started teaching seven years ago, we did frog dissections at the end of the year. I thought it would be prudent of me to email all the parents to let them know this would be happening. The day after I sent the email, I went into town to grab a coffee and saw a few new fliers on the bulletin board outside the cafe.

As I got closer and read them, I was both annoyed and cracking up at what this flier was all about. The title of the leaflet read, "Local middle school teacher murdering frogs in the name of science!" Below that was a long letter to the community telling them how horrible I was for allowing the community's children to endure the horrific practice of frog dissections. This person, who was the mother of one of my "most favorite students" (insert sarcasm here) also called the local water district and told them I was dumping formaldehyde into storm drains and disposing of sharps inappropriately, neither of which was true.

I had a lot of hoops to jump through and nerves to calm

at the local water district for the first few weeks of summer, while trying to convince everyone in the community that I didn't compromise the safety of their water supply!

45

TF GOING ON BRUH

can you change my grade i had a whole 90 sum and i did my rough draft and i showwd you and you put a zero like tf goiñ on bruh rs cause i did all of that the draft i showed that oi was doin it

46

GRANDPA IS DEAD, SEE?

ANONYMOUS

I was a relatively new music teacher, and I was conducting auditions for a concert. I had signups for students to audition for a solo piece. I had the signup sheet posted for two weeks and held auditions during lunch for a week. On Saturday, a week after auditions were over, I got an email from a student politely asking if she could still audition since she was absent on the last day of tryouts. As nicely as I could, I explained that the deadline had passed and that she hadn't signed up to indicate interest. It would be unfair to others.

That Monday, I received an email from the student's mother that read, "Before you pass JUDGEMENT and PENANCE, you should know what is going on in our family." She went on to explain that her husband had been diagnosed with cancer that week, and that her daughter's grandfather had just passed away. That is why she wasn't in school during audition week or on Friday.

I scrolled to the bottom of the email and saw an enormous picture of a dead man in a coffin. She had sent me a picture of the deceased grandfather.

After I picked my jaw up off the floor, I forwarded the email to my supervisor and politely asked how to handle the situation. Five minutes later the phone rings, and my supervisor asks me, "What the fuck is that?" All I could reply with was, "My student's dead grandfather... I think."

My supervisor supported my decision in not allowing the girl to audition. Rules are rules.

The girl came to school the next day, and I told her I was sorry to hear about her father's cancer and her grandfather's death and gave my sympathies. Her response? "My dad is going to be fine. They caught it early last year, and it's totally treatable. My grandfather's not dead. He lives in Cuba, and I've never met him before. Who told you that?"

I just smiled and said, "Never mind."

YOU NEED A SNICKERS BAR

i dident do anything

To You

2:42 PM

000

I didn't do anything I was just standing you really need to eat a snickers bar any I was talking when the bell was finna ring and you almost made me late and you acted like everything was my falt that's messed up you yelled at me 10 times I counted miss explain this it wasent my falt miss say sorry you almost ruined my perfect record and you keep on acting sarcastic what a surprise I have feeling you you just cut me off like that that's rude and you should say sorry I'm very disappointed in how you acted😐

WHOSE EYE IS THIS?

BRITTANY, PENNSYLVANIA

My first year of teaching special education was quite a year. I had a little girl with a glass eye, and her mother warned me that she often pops it out when she's bored. Luckily, she never did it during class, but one day after school, I got a text from her mom that said, "Hey, have you seen Edna's eye?"

I immediately started a frantic search in the classroom and playground, but I couldn't find her eye. Eventually, I called the bus driver who said, "Oh, I didn't know that was someone's eye. I saw Billy had it in his mouth and figured it was his, so I stuck it in his backpack."

I sent a message to Billy's mom that said, "Hello! The bus driver put something in Billy's backpack today. It was something from another student. It's her glass eye. Can you stick it in a baggie and send it back tomorrow? Thanks!" The eye was returned the next day and was hopefully disinfected!

OK THEN!

Hello! I am Mrs. Rodriguez, and I am your student's French 1 teacher. I am very excited to work with your student this year! If you would like to contact me, please email ▬▬

g . I hope to see you for Open School Night on ▬▬ Thanks!

Fuck off

TWO I'LL NEVER FORGET

ANONYMOUS

I HAD A 10TH-GRADE STUDENT WHO WAS ALWAYS IN trouble. He usually went to in-school suspension (ISS) twice a week. One day he came into class and told us all that his girlfriend was pregnant and he's the dad. Everyone in the class started laughing at him and telling him that he was going to be a terrible father because he couldn't stay out of trouble. I could see that it was really getting to him. Right then, I stopped the class and made a deal with him. If he could stay out of trouble for his entire junior year, I would buy him a cake. He didn't have much, so this was an excellent prize for him. I didn't even think about a price limit for the cake, but he decided on no more than $50.

We created a contract, both signed it, and I hung it up at the front of my room for everyone to see. It was easy to keep up with his behavior or trips to ISS because every teacher got a list of students in ISS every day. During his junior year, he would send me pictures of cakes he wanted, and I just put them in a special folder for when/if the time came. Sure enough, he made it all year without getting in trouble, but he could never decide on a cake. I ended up buying him my favorite: Great American Cookie. I bought the biggest cake I could buy for $50. When he came to my class to get his cake, he was almost brought to tears and truly didn't believe that I bought him a cake. He told me to take half of it, but I made him take it all and give it to whomever he wanted because he had earned it.

We decided to do it again his senior year, this time it was for a $100 gift card for his senior trip. He made it through his senior year without getting in trouble, and when I found him at graduation, he told me that he couldn't accept the gift card because he had fussed at a teacher two days prior and spent half a day in ISS. I made him take the card because he came clean. At the beginning of his sophomore year, he would have lied like crazy to get that money, but he came clean to me, admitting that he had gotten in trouble, and that meant more to me than anything.

I had a 9th-grade student named Brandon who was poor as dirt. He rarely took a shower and wore the same clothes every day. He wanted any kind of attention he could get—mostly playing dumb to get some laughs from the class. My coworkers called him my child because he had the same hair color as me, and he was always in my room asking questions or just wanting somewhere to be. He didn't have any friends and ate breakfast and lunch with the cafeteria workers. After two years with him though, he had a special place in my heart.

He always freaked out when he was going to miss a day of school, and wanted to know what he needed to do to get caught up or stay ahead. One day during his 10th-grade year, he came to me to tell me that he was going to miss school the following Friday. I asked him where he was going to be. He told me that he had an interview with 12 For Life. 12 For Life is a program run by Southwire (a company in Carroll County, GA) that takes at-risk kids (at risk of failing, dropping out, or kids who may not have a chance to go to a tech school or college) and trains them to work at Southwire. The kids go to their home school and then are bused, if needed, to Southwire. When kids are accepted into the program, they take their core classes there, and they get paid! I was so excited when he told me that he had an interview.

Wanting so badly for him to get the job, I asked him what he was going to wear. He told me jeans and a t-shirt. I told him that that wasn't appropriate interview attire. I learned that he didn't own a comb or decent shoes. I got his sizes and went to Walmart to buy him new clothes. He was 16 years old at the time and still wearing junior size clothes. I got him some khakis, shoes, and a shirt/clip-on tie combo. The next day I told him to come to my room during lunch to try on his clothes. He went to the restroom to try it on and came out so that I could see if they fit. Bless his heart, the buttons were buttoned crookedly. I made sure to remind him to button them correctly, but everything else looked great, including the smile on his face.

A few weeks later, he told me that he got the job, but he would be taking Biology (my class) at Southwire. I was heartbroken but knew it would be best for him. My parents always told me to save half of my paycheck and put it in savings. I passed that information along to him but told him to blow his first paycheck on whatever he wanted. If he wanted a new game or gaming system, buy it. Whatever he wanted, he deserved.

I hadn't seen him in weeks. Finally, he came to my room to check in, and we caught up on his new job. During our conversation, I asked him what he had spent his first paycheck on, expecting to hear that he had bought a PlayStation. Nope. He told me that he took his parents to Longhorn Steakhouse for a nice dinner. I started crying right there. He could have bought anything (within reason), and he chose to take his parents out to dinner.

I have since moved and don't teach at that school anymore, but one of my friends who still teaches there found Brandon at graduation, took a picture of him, and sent it to me. I have never felt more proud of any student.

EXCUSE ME WHILE I FILE THIS
RESTRAINING ORDER

Dear MS. Reid I'm
Sorry for saving I'm
gonna Scratch Your eyes
out and Put it in
Your ass I wont ever
cause or Say that again
I'm Sorry for hurting Your
feeling

52

GET OVER YOURSELF

CHRISTINE O., NEW JERSEY

My first job teaching art was at the school I went to from kindergarten through eighth grade. I was the youngest person on staff by 13 years. My coworkers were my old teachers who I had always looked up to. I felt safe and reassured that they would help me transition into teaching.

They treated me so horribly and I had such a bad experience there, that I wound up changing jobs to escape it. One kept pestering me to do a lesson about fossils with her fifth-grade class. I had lesson plans and a curriculum I was getting accustomed to, so I delayed her request. She started to call me "Fossil Girl" every time she saw me. Even though she was my fifth-grade teacher, she began to bully me.

The principal, who was my principal when I was younger and was actually supportive, found out that this teacher was bullying me and confronted her. The shit hit the fan big time!

Most of the teachers rallied around the other teacher and made me feel very uncomfortable constantly. I traveled between two schools to teach art, and the middle school teachers (who also taught me in middle school) sided with the other teacher as well. I went to the president of the union. She shrugged her shoulders and said it is what it is.

Come spring, I was told I was in charge of the eighth grade graduation decorations. The man who ran graduation couldn't handle it. It was his 30th year running it, but it still made him dizzy. I tried everything to figure out what exactly I was supposed to prepare for graduation but never got a straight answer. I emailed, sent notes, and popped in to his class, but I never got an answer as to what decorations I was supposed to supply.

The days ticked by so I went to another eighth grade teacher who had been an ally up till this day. I asked her what decorations she thought I should prepare for graduation. She snapped her head back and forth in a rant saying, "Graduation is *not* about *you*! Your questions are *meaningless* and *annoying*! Art is a non-tested subject!" I started to crumble and tears welled up in my eyes as she added, "No one cares about you! Get *over* yourself and oh God! Quit crying!"

Everyone at work was invited to the retirement party of my former science teacher, except me. My parents were friends with her and I've known her my whole life, but still, I wasn't included.

I was outside of my classroom hanging projects when she approached me the week of her party. I thought, "Here we go, a pity invite... Or maybe she totally forgot to invite me!" She said, "I know you are in need of money. I thought it would be nice if you could be a waitress at my retirement party. I'll pay you."

I don't understand why they treated me that way, but it led me to give up on teaching for a while. Four years later I started teaching at the high school I went to. My past teachers surrounded me with love and encouragement. It has been a wonderful experience but I'm still a little scarred from my first year of teaching.

53

A LIFESTYLE CHOICE

To: School Nurse
From: 3rd Grade Teacher
Subject: Lice Concern

Hello. I am writing to ask about the school policy regarding lice. I have a student who has a lot of nits, and I sent her to you, but she was sent right back. Were her parents contacted? Is it OK to send a message home to the parents of the other students to warn them of the presence of lice in the classroom? Please advise!

To: 3rd Grade Teacher
From: School Nurse
Subject: Re: Lice Concern

As crazy as this may sound, we cannot contact the student's parents because she only has nits. You also cannot contact any other parents. You

can ask administration for a copy of what the
policy is regarding lice to see the specifics. I just
do what I am told. This is the district policy.
Lice is kind of like for lack of a better term a
"lifestyle choice." Some parents are diligent
about lice and others are not. It is expensive to
treat lice and many families cannot afford treatment. Also lice is now resistant to many over-
the-counter treatments and needs to be treated
with a prescription medication in most cases.
Trust me, I feel your frustration but we really
need to have students in school. They are
allowed to have nits but no live bugs. If a
student comes to me with nits but I don't see
anything live, the student goes right back to
class. I hope this answers some of your
concerns.

54

WHO RAISES THEM

E.J., COLUMBIA, MO

HAVE YOU EVER HAD A STUDENT WHO WAS SO ANGRY and out of control that you kept wondering what their life must be like at home? Well, I did some home visits, and it's worse than you can imagine.

I used to teach Title 1 Pre-K. I taught summer school for kindergarten children who had failed. It was our job to catch them up so they'd be ready for first grade. Little "Wilma" was 6 years old and very difficult. She was short-tempered and mouthy, often talking back to the teachers, as well as any other student who crossed her. One day she had an exceptionally angry blow-up and threatened to bring her machine gun to school and shoot us all to death. Yikes. I took her kicking and screaming to the office, where we waited for the principal for over an hour. She eventually calmed down but cried hysterically that she was so tired. Why? Her grandmother (who was her guardian) was also a nurse and daycare provider. She babysat other nurses' children at night while they worked, but if she was working, six-year-old Wilma and her ten-year-old brother were in charge of the six babies their grandma babysat at night! The night before, Wilma had been up nearly all night taking care of the babies– heating bottles, changing diapers, rocking and comforting tiny babies– all while her ten-year-old brother was watching Def Comedy Jam at full volume (keeping the babies and Wilma from sleeping.) I wanted to bundle that little girl up in my arms and take her home with me.

The program I taught in the fall consisted of four days a week of Pre-K with Fridays off for home visits to bring a book and do some parent education in the students' homes. Some places were so unhealthy or downright dangerous that we had to go in small groups. Two places stand out: the first had two preschoolers and at least half a dozen school-aged children living there. We arrived to consult with the mother and visit the children and found lunchtime happening. Taco Bell was on the coffee table for the children and adults to swing by and grab a bite as they went about their day. That didn't seem too bad, but then almost a dozen cats came in, helping themselves to the Taco Bell amongst the children and adults. There were cat paws that had just been in the litter box, stepping on burritos that the three-year-old was also picking up to nibble. Cat mouths that had recently been outside eating a dead bird were now licking the sour cream from the taco that was eaten by the five-year-old. Then the dad walked through the room with his hands full of raw steaks. Mom asked what he was up to, and he reminded her that it was time to train the fighting pit bulls.

Again, I wanted to put those children in my car and get them out of that house.

Those were the relatively safe houses. There were others where drug deals were going on in the backroom or possibly in the driveway. And several where the moms were high as a kite, alone at home with small children and babies. Nothing was done when reported to the district– safe zone my arse. Those babies have grown up and are probably repeating the cycle, if they lived through it.

As for me? I quit years ago and homeschool my kids. I'm happy to remain in my bubble, far away from public school!

55

WHO RAISES THEM PART 2

STEPHANIE JONES, ATLANTA, GEORGIA

BEFORE I BECAME A FULL TIME TEACHER I WORKED AS a tutor. One day, my superior told me that I would be going to a "rough" neighborhood. The directions I was given were something along the lines of, "Get off the highway exit, make a right, pass the burnt down apartment complex, then turn left at the drive-thru liquor store and hook a right when you pass the second condemned apartment complex."

From a distance, the house looked structurally sound. It had a roof, and the stairs leading to the porch were all there. The driveway contained nearly a twelve-pack of forty-ounce beer bottles, a few hundred cigarette butts, and three crack torch lighters. The little boy who answered the door simply opened it and walked away. Stepping into the stifling heat, I adjusted my gaze and looked for a guardian. I saw her on the phone in another room, and she pointed at the little girl I was there to assess.

"Hi there! I am here to assess you for your tutorials. I understand you are in the sixth grade. How was your day today at school?"

She just blinked and stared at me.

"So, how about we go ahead and get started, okay?"

I asked her if she would like to take the test in her room, and she shook her head. Looking around the place, I was hard-pressed to find a table or suitable "learning environment." There was no couch or table, just a single chair and a dusty beanbag in the corner. The little girl trailed off into the darkness at the end of the hallway. She returned with a single chair, sat down in it, and mumbled, "I'm ready."

I gave her the assessment. It had about 100 questions on it, fifty for math and fifty for language arts. Students typically need an entire two hours to take it, and while they answer the questions, tutors usually try to get to know the parents, in the hopes that they might convince them to tote their child across town to meet, instead of having to go across town to meet them. There was no parent for me to ham it up with. She was still, presumably, on the phone.

I looked around for a place to sit and decided on the dusty beanbag. I pulled out my computer and started typing nervously, creating a report for another student of mine. Suddenly I had to pee very badly. Earlier I had resolved to drink three liters of water before the day was out, which was a pretty stupid idea.

"Hey, mind if I use your bathroom?" I asked. She shook her head and pointed. I headed towards the bathroom and immediately checked for toilet tissue, but there was none.

I didn't want to disturb the woman on the phone, so I knocked on a closed door near the bathroom. The little boy who opened the front door popped his head out. "Hello again," I said. "Do you have some toilet tissue?" He blinked but said nothing. I repeated, "Do you have some toilet tissue?" He said he would check and closed the door. I waited for a while until it became clear that the little boy was not coming back.

I decided to hover and use the drip-dry method. I closed the door and released a stream of urine Sea Biscuit would have been proud of. I hovered and glanced around the bathroom and saw that the wallpaper was decorated with oddly sized brown dots. I wasn't wearing my glasses. I thought the pattern was strange but became distracted while trying to shake off residual urine with minimal spatter. Feeling that not so fresh feeling, I began washing my hands and looked in the mirror. One of the dots on the wallpaper suddenly began to move across the wall approaching the mirror. The dot was alive! It had six legs and would make a repulsive yet satisfying crunch if squished. There were about a thousand of these dots in the tiny bathroom, scurrying around.

The sheer number of roaches inhabiting the bathroom was overwhelming. I walked out, sat back in the beanbag chair, and continued to type. I looked over at my new student taking her assessment, praying to God that she passed it so I would never have to return. I had to come up with a good plan of escape. I briefly considered forgery and wondered how I could make the test look as if it took her some time to complete because she made a few mistakes, but not so many that she failed. As I was contemplating all of this, I noticed more moving roaches on the carpet. Again, the dots varied in size and speed, but they were all moving, which meant they were alive. I wanted to get up and walk around and make sure that no part of me touched the ground longer than a couple of seconds so that none of them could jump on me and crawl up my legs.

I decided to go outside and call my boss. I figured she would know what to do because she trained me, and she would know the proper protocol.

"Stephanie, what's the problem, dear?" my boss asked, sounding slightly irritated.

"I am at the house you sent me to, and I am giving the assessment, but I have to go! There are like millions of roaches in the house with us, and I have to go! I left my purse in there! Oh God, they are probably setting up tents and shit all over my stuff! I have to get out of here!"

"What?" my boss replied.

"Are you listening to me?" I tried to yell loud enough for her to hear me but quietly enough that the family wouldn't understand. "There are roaches inside the house! There are lots of them, they are everywhere, on the floor, on the walls, just hanging out! I went to the bathroom, and there were all stages of life represented on the walls. There were baby roaches, teens, adults, geriatric roaches that had like only five out of the six working legs! Seriously! Get me the fuck outta here! I don't care if that little girl scores a six percent and deserves extra hours, I can't do this!"

There was silence while my boss tried to hold back her laughter, and after about seven seconds, the dam burst. I noticed that there wasn't just one laugh track, but several laugh tracks played in the background. I was on speaker-phone, and the whole office was laughing.

"They are everywhere!" I pleaded, trying to express the seriousness of the situation. "Stephanie, is she almost done with the assessment?" she asked.

"Are you kidding me? I could give a fuck! I am leaving! Someone else can do this!"

I ran back into the house to gather my things. "Are you done yet?" I asked the girl. I looked at her progress; there were lots of doodles on her test. She had only answered four questions. My anxiety took over. "Here, let me see that! Yup, this will do. Awesome! You did awesome!" I felt bad for her, but I just couldn't stay.

I took the test and shook it out a bit. "Now, I must talk

to your mother and tell her how wonderful you did." The little girl stared at me, she hesitated and then decided to play along. She knew she answered four out of fifty questions, and I was simply lying to her face about her awesomeness. "I'll be right back," she said and disappeared.

I slowly inspected my things and started to pack them when something moved behind the door of the dimly lit room. I froze and heard a shuffling and dragging noise. I started to get freaked out. A man with a claw-like hand at the end of his arm shuffled out into the light. He was almost entirely bent over and dragged one of his legs like it weighed a thousand pounds. He just stood there and stared at me, though he was almost completely cross-eyed. I assumed this was the girl's dad.

"Hello," I said. "I am here to assess your daughter for school. She is done with her test, so I'll be right on my way."

"Her mom is in there on the phone. How'd she do? She half stupid, you know. She don't do right with reading and all that."

"Umm, these are just preliminary results, but I am hopeful." A baby started crying from the darkness.

"That's my son. He's two months old. Wanna see him?" He asked. "No, I'm just getting over a cold. I wouldn't want to get him sick or anything," I answered.

"Who you talking to out there? Is that the tutor?" the mom called out.

"Yeah, she say she got test scores, and she wanna talk to you," he yelled back.

"Hi!" I said as the mom entered the room.

"I'm so glad you're here!" mom responded. "She don't do right in reading. You know she was held back a grade."

"Well, the office will look over these tests, and they will assign a proper learning path. So if you could just sign these papers, I can drop her scores off at the office, and we can get started!"

"Sure! She really needs help! I want her to have all the help she can get."

I tried to change my view of the situation. Economic hard times fall indiscriminately, and who am I to judge the worth of a person based on income? I wanted to help their daughter, but I couldn't do it there.

"Thank you so much for coming out today! We gonna look for you soon!" she said as I folded the papers in half, stuffed them in my bag, and placed my hand on the door.

"Yes! I am so excited as well!" I lied, and turned the knob, leaping down the stairs upon its closure.

"You can't come in this house!" my mom said after listening to my horror story.

"What? Mom! I need to shower and get this day off of my body!"

"Well, you are going to have to take all of your clothes off in the garage. I will wait there for you to shake your clothes out, and we can put them directly into the washer. I will have a towel for you, and while you undress, I will look through your hair."

"Mom, are you serious? I shook out all my stuff already."

Sure enough, I pulled into the garage, and my mother was standing in the doorway with a towel and a comb. She made me take off all of my clothes and went through my hair, looking for bugs.

Against all pleading and begging to my boss, I was told that I would have to keep tutoring the student at her house and could simply wear biohazard jumpsuits to our meetings, which she would provide. I called the number listed on the student's intake forms, and the number had been disconnected. I was relieved but sad at the same time.

SIGNIFICANT FEEDBACK

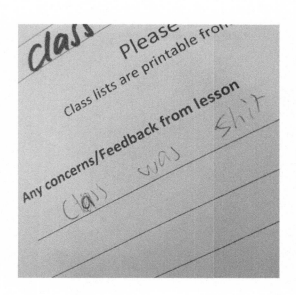

OH SHITBALLS

AMANDA, TAMPA, FLORIDA

ONE YEAR I WAS THE SUPERVISING TEACHER FOR A teaching intern. Early on, it became clear that she struggled with classroom management. We tried many different strategies to help her gain control, but the class was disrespectful, and she started to dread coming to work.

Towards the end of the school year, she was becoming disillusioned and was considering leaving teaching altogether. I felt terrible because I wanted to help her so much, but I just had no idea what else to do for her. One day she was venting to me about her day when she said, "I just don't know why they keep leaving shit around." I thought she meant they were leaving their things out, and I told her that fifth graders are just naturally slobs. That's when she looked at me and told me that I was mistaken.

They were actually leaving *balls of shit* on her whiteboard tray! I was shocked! I asked her what the principal had said when she told her. Surely parents had been told, and these children were being suspended at least, but nope! She never told admin about it because she didn't want it to reflect poorly on her that her students were so out of control that they were leaving shitballs around the class for her.

Never in my life did I think I would have to explain to someone that kids that roll poop balls and leave them for the teacher should be punished. It's crazy what kids get away with these days.

SAVING MY DAUGHTER FROM MATH

to me

Dec 14 View details

Dear
 I'm deeply sorry for calling my daughter
during math class. I knew her schedule and
saw she was in math class and thought that
it would be the best time to call her
because according to me,(no offense) math
is irrelevant. The world would be a much
better place without it. I couldn't stand to
see my daughter suffering in math so I
knew I had to save her by calling her. Please
don't be mad at her it was my fault.

Sincerely,

CALL 911! MY DAUGHTER LOST A TOOTH!

ANONYMOUS, MIAMI, FLORIDA

I WAS TEACHING FIRST GRADE IN FLORIDA AND ONE OF my students lost her tooth. This is a pretty regular occurrence in first grade, and I handled it the way I always did. She was given a little baggie for her tooth, and I let her wash her mouth out in the sink. Naturally she had a bit of blood, but we cleaned it, and all seemed fine.

Soon after we went to dismissal, where the little girl proudly told her mother of her lost tooth. The following day I was summoned by the principal who ushered me into his office and closed the door. He was furious and demanded to know why I didn't *call fire rescue* for the child who lost her tooth yesterday. I was in shock. The mother called him and complained that her daughter was bleeding at school, and I didn't call her immediately. The principal sided with the mother and demanded I apologize. He reiterated that I should have called fire rescue and finished by saying that if he were the parent, he would call the state and have my teaching license revoked.

This story is 100% true, and there's nothing more to it.

You'd think for him to be that upset, there would be more to the story. But there isn't.

LIKE A DOG WHO SEES A SQUIRREL

We do have adults out front and in the cafeteria reminding. I can remind him as well.

I expect him to make it to breakfast, if that means an adult gathers up breakfast kids and walls them to the cafeteria that's kinda what I expect. He's in kindergarten, if he has been in school a few years and costs to forget that'd on him. At this point we're talking about a scenario with a dog that's hungry and on its way to the food bowl, but sees a squirrel.

AC

61

ATTACK OF THE VIBRATING BACKPACK

ANONYMOUS

I TEACH JUNIOR HIGH, SO I'VE SEEN MY FAIR SHARE OF odd trends, but this one sticks out in particular. I was in my second year of teaching. Cell phones were becoming more of a problem, so our school enacted a new policy– if you see it or hear it– take it, and the student will pick it up from the teacher at the end of the day. One day, as the bell rang, I heard a buzzing coming from a student's bag. I sighed and turned around to see the most mortified face on a fourteen-year-old boy I've ever seen. His jaw was clenched, his hands were trembling, and his eyes could be described as that of a startled owl on opioids. I gave him an exasperated look as his 30 classmates took notice of the situation that was developing. I thrust out my hand and said, "Okay, Chester, you know the drill. Turn it over."

Chester turned pale and froze. The class started to giggle nervously. "Hand it over," I repeated, a bit annoyed at this point.

Chester was still frozen in fear. Meanwhile, the bag was buzzing away. In fact, it hadn't stopped the whole time. There was no rhythm to the buzzing either– just a loud continual hum. It dawned on me then that this might not be a phone buzzing. I closed my hand, dropped my voice, and said to the petrified Chester, "Go to the office and hand over the bag to an administrator." I walked him to the door and asked a nearby coworker to escort him to the office. About three hours later, I learned that I had made the right call. Chester didn't have a phone or a blackberry, but he did have a big black vibrating dildo in his bag.

I was asking him to "hand it over," and it turns out I was asking him to give me a huge vibrating penis in the middle of a group of crazed middle schoolers. This was the day I learned that there must be exceptions to every rule.

Chester got suspended for bringing this "toy" to school, but it didn't stop with him. A week later, another teacher heard the infamous buzzing in her class from another student's bag. That's right! It was another vibrator. Apparently, a group of boys was bringing them to school as some sort of game. The takeaway: if something is buzzing without a pause, just throw the bag into the hallway and do not, under any circumstances, ask the student to take the item out for all to see!

YOUR STUPID BREASTMILK

From: Aquaria's mom
Subject: Lunchtime concern

Good afternoon.
My daughter came home very distraught yester-
day. She was almost in tears as she told me that
her lunch time that she has with all of her
friends was taken away, yet again, due to you
having to pump breast milk for your newborn
child at the beginning of the class period. As I
mother myself I understand the importance of
breast milk but also as a mother it is important
to me that my child is happy at school. Since
this activity takes 15 minutes, could you
perhaps consider doing that at a different time
so that my daughter and her friends can have
the lunch time they originally had? I am not
only speaking for my daughter. I also speak on
behalf of other parents who have the same

**concern as I. I appreciate your understanding
in this important matter.**

CHASING GUNTHER

JULIE PERRY, TALLAHASSEE, FLORIDA

I GRADUATED COLLEGE WITH A DUAL DEGREE IN Elementary Ed. and Exceptional Student Ed. I was hired three weeks after graduation by a public middle school in the poorest part of the city. I wasn't deterred by the fact that it was middle school, or that the school was known for severe behavior problems. I was young and idealistic and was determined to change the world for the better.

The job I landed was called "Community Based Instruction." I would be teaching grades 6-8, all kids with varying intellectual and physical disabilities who were on a special diploma track. I was excited about this because I got the dual major specifically to work with kids with disabilities, which I thought was my great calling in life. I was to start my job in January, halfway through the school year. I would be replacing a thirty year veteran teacher who had retired partway through the year, or so I was told. It wasn't until I had been there a few weeks that I found out there had already been two teachers before me who had tried and failed, miserably, to take the original teacher's place. One, I heard, quit when a particular kid snatched the wig off of her head and threw it into the woods in retaliation for her confiscating his phone. The same kid would later go on to curse me out daily, once even asking me if I was "fucking" the young male paraprofessional who helped in my classroom.

In this class, I had sixteen profoundly disabled students of varying capabilities for which I was expected to create a curriculum. As I learned, much to my dismay, the teacher before me had simply given them packets of spelling lists and word searches to do all day. I was young, inspired, and optimistic, and therefore set about killing myself, working 12-14 hour days to create individualized curriculums for each kid. There was one major problem, however, that got in the way of learning, despite my valiant efforts. I'll call him "Gunther."

Gunther was a 14-year-old male who was severely intellectually disabled. He also had verbal apraxia. You can imagine his frustration because he struggled to communicate much of anything at all. As a result, Gunther resorted to bathroom accidents, nudity, and violence to express his frustration. I had to go to specialized training to learn to restrain Gunther "safely" when he became a danger to himself or the other kids, whom, unfortunately, he attacked frequently. Gunther was also a runner. This presented a serious issue because my classroom was located by the parking lot, which was connected to a busy road. So each day, at least once, if not multiple times a day, I was either restraining Gunther, throwing off my high heels to chase him out the door and through the parking lot before he made it to the road, or both. There was one day in particular, though, that I will never forget. It is one of the hallmark moments of my teaching career and has helped to shape me into the weathered, strict, and "savage" (as the kids say) teacher that I am today.

Gunther started having major accidents in his pants regularly. On this particular day, he had an accident and decided that he was not going to wait to be changed, but proceeded to rip all of his clothes off and run, completely naked, out the door. I promptly yelled to my para to radio admin, threw off my heels, and flew out the door after him. Gunther was clearly having an adrenaline rush, and I was having trouble catching up to him. Very soon, however, the principal, the assistant principal, and the Dean of Discipline had all joined me in the chase. All three of us chased him, in all his naked glory, around the parking lot until eventually we caught him. But not before garnering an audience of students. This meant a mountain of paperwork and a legal nightmare for the school.

I worked in that school for three more years before realizing that I wasn't going to make it 27 more in that environment and that maybe teaching English was my true calling after all. When I tell this story, people always ask how I'm still teaching and what made me stay. I don't really have a good answer to that question, other than that it's all I ever saw myself doing, and despite the stress, there was something about it I loved, and still do to this day. Somehow, 10 years later, I can look back and laugh about my first few years of teaching.

MY KID SUCKS. CAN HE BE EXCUSED FOR THAT?

? Inbox ☆

to me

11:51 AM View details

Hello,

So every morning is pure HE double hockey sticks to get ▇▇▇ to go to school, and every day he's been getting dismissed....can he be done for the rest of the year?

Please let me know!

LIFE IS BUT A DREAM

ANONYMOUS

I HAD A PARENT SEND ME AN EMAIL LAST YEAR SAYING that she was going to call the cops and have me investigated. She said no one had ever treated her son so poorly, and I should be ashamed to call myself a teacher. I was astonished. I had no idea what might make her think such a thing.

The principal contacted her to ask what happened, and she said her son had a bad dream about me and was very upset in his sleep. She felt that he wouldn't have had such a vivid dream if I hadn't been treating him poorly in class. The principal took a long time to explain that dreams are not necessarily related to any real events and that I am an excellent teacher. Then she said that she didn't have a problem with me and agreed I was a good teacher. She never apologized.

THANKS BUT NO THANKS

thank you For All
the extra work that
I really Don't Do and
it Bringing my Grade
Down So i would
Appreciate it iF
you would lighten
UP with the work

But thanks For
everything eles

FLOYD'S LITTLE DISCOVERY

LAURA M., MIAMI, FLORIDA

THREE YEARS AGO, I WAS TEACHING A CLASS OF SECOND-grade "gifted" students. I put that in quotations because the psychologist we had assigned to us was about 108 years old and believed every damn child that she saw was gifted, but that's beside the point. That year I had a particular student (we'll call him Floyd) who was probably one of the biggest asshole kids I have ever taught. He thought he was the smartest, funniest kid in the world, and of course, his parents agreed (insert massive eye roll). Even teachers who observed my class would ask, "Who's that asshole?" because he would give the creepiest, grossest looks to all the female teachers.

One day I was in the middle of a lesson, and I looked over at Floyd (his desk was an "island" because he could not get along with any other human being), and I saw him shaking vigorously. I stopped and asked him if he was okay. Perhaps he needed to go to the bathroom? He said he was fine, and the shaking stopped. The next day as I was teaching in front of the room it happened again. I stopped, glanced around his desk, and asked him again if he was okay. He said he was fine, so I reminded him to stop playing around.

That night I received a message from another student's mom (who sat near Floyd) telling me that her son saw Floyd take his penis out of his pants under his desk and was masturbating! I teach no older than second grade for a reason. I have no interest in dealing with horny kids, and I never expected to have to deal with a masturbating seven-year-old!

It turns out that Floyd watched porn on another kid's phone during his Before Care program and thought he'd try that shit out in my class! (Since some of you might be thinking he was abused or had something traumatic happen to him, I can assure you there was no evidence of that.)

Of course, we had to call a meeting with the parents. Their immediate response was, "That cannot possibly be! The other kid is lying!" We called Floyd into the meeting and grilled him in front of the parents until he admitted it. He said that the kids in his Before Care program showed him porn, and he started thinking about it in class and got really excited and thought no one would notice. His parents looked like they wanted to curl up and die. Then they tried to blame the other kids for introducing him to porn. I don't think it's a coincidence that they moved out of state shortly after.

HAPPY TO HELP

DON'T MESS WITH MOM

MS. B, BRIDGEPORT, CONNECTICUT

I TAUGHT FIRST GRADE IN AN INNER-CITY SCHOOL FOR one year. It was a Pre-K through 8 bilingual school with approximately 985 students. We had a wide range of ages in our school because parents didn't know what grade to place their children in and kids were often held back; one of our eighth graders was 16 years old.

The area our school was in had a high rate of gang affiliation. There were fifth graders with teardrop tattoos on their faces (indicating they had either murdered or attempted to kill someone). We would go into lockdowns at least once a day, sometimes more often, because kids would be found with weapons on them or because of nasty fights.

One early spring day right after my first-grade team finished dismissing our students, a partial lockdown was called due to an altercation in front of the building. One of my grade partners and I looked out of her front-facing window and saw the mother of one of my first-grade students involved in a horrible fight with a sixth-grade girl. We watched as the mother pounded this student's head into the concrete sidewalk, a giant puddle of blood forming on the ground around them. The security guards in our building didn't keep weapons on them, but when one of them tried to break it up, she was accidentally stabbed in the arm with a paintbrush that had been chiseled into a shank. Eventually, the police arrived and were able to break up the fight.

The girl was reported to be in critical condition and didn't return to school for the rest of the year. She lived through the fight, but we were told that she ended up with some brain damage. The mother was arrested, but no one was willing to testify against her due to her gang affiliation. She was released about a month later. Her son, who was in my first-grade class at the time, stayed in school for the following week but was then relocated to live with his grandmother in another state.

aye bro unmarked me from
tardy bruh like for real Kids

71

RULES AND REGULATIONS

ANONYMOUS

A FEW YEARS AGO, WE HAD A MIDDLE SCHOOL STUDENT who stole another student's water bottle out of his backpack, then snuck it into the bathroom and urinated into it. He then returned to the classroom, took out the urine-filled bottle, and poured it onto several of the desks! He even rubbed his hands in it and smeared some onto his face as well before tossing the bottle in the trash. The entire room had to be cleared, students in the hallway, etc. An administrator came, but another teacher had to put on gloves and retrieve the bottle from the garbage so the administrator could smell it to prove it was, in fact, urine.

The consequences, you ask? *None.*

The administration tried to suspend the student, but the superintendent refused, claiming there's nothing about urination in the district's rules & regulations.

THAT'S A HIGH BAR

Dear Mrs. Store
You are the
best music
teacher's ever
because my
last music teacher
choked a boy.

love your student,

A MORE LOVING TEACHER

ANONYMOUS

MY FIFTH-GRADE CLASS HAD BEEN WORKING ON A BOOK report for a month. Two weeks before it was due, I got a visit from the principal. Herbert's mom wanted to know why I was making her baby cry. She said it had been happening all year, though he was always happy and had never cried in class. The principal told me to do whatever I had to do to make him happy. (Huh?) A week later, the principal emailed me and said, "Herbert couldn't do his work, because you refused to let him have a pencil in class. Is this true?" I explained that of course, it was not true. A week later I received another email that said, "Herbert's mom feels that you are prejudiced against red hair. You wouldn't single him out, would you?" At this point, I was just laughing because the accusation was so ridiculous. I recalled how coworkers had told me that the principal was weak and afraid of confrontation with parents.

A week before the due date of the report, Herbert's dad came to my room with his son after school. He asked if we had a book report due next week. I told him that we did. He said his child didn't have a book because I didn't allow him to get one. I explained that he *did* have a book. I issued it to him before Christmas. His son had told me that he read it over the break and has had it in class while working on his draft. The dad looked at his child who turned red and began to apologize for lying to get out of doing homework. His dad said, "You had mom and I thinking your teacher was some mean old hag." We talked about everything. How Herbert had pencils every day, my liking his red hair, and how he never typed more than two sentences on a given day, etc. I thought we were on the same page.

On the day the rough draft of the book report was due, Herbert entered with a complete, immaculately typed book report in hand. I said, "Wow, this is great! You are so lucky to have parents who care about you. I'm so glad they helped you practice typing your book report." We began typing and editing final drafts. Herbert was done with his five-paragraph paper (with perfect grammar and spelling) in 10 pecks of the keyboard. It was an exact replica of the first. I manually checked his google documents and low and behold, mom had emailed him a copy. I explained to him that this is something he had to do on his own. Although class time was over, I would give him another chance if he wanted to give up his recess and/or gym time.

Herbert used his iPhone to call his mom at recess instead. Soon after the principal appeared in my doorway. He was cackling and wringing his hands together. He wanted a play-by-play of what took place with Herbert. After I explained, his reply was, "Be more proactive with the parents!" and that was that.

After school, I called home. There was no answer. I left a voicemail. I called the second number. Dad answered. I asked if he had a moment. I began to explain the situation and why it was important for Herbert to do his work on his own. I also told him if it wasn't completed by the end of the week, it would result in a zero. I volunteered to stay and help Herbert if they could pick him up an hour later than usual. Dad called me a fucking bitch, a manipulative cunt, and a motherfucker. He told me that I *would* give his son the grade that paper deserved because he and his wife didn't read that *fucking book* and stay up *all fucking night* doing that report for nothing! Then he threatened that if I didn't give his son an A, he would come up to the school and "take care of me." (Keep in mind he was on speaker-phone in front of the secretary and the counselor.) I hung up. I had done nothing wrong. The principal was gone for the day and unreachable, so I typed up what had happened.

The following day, I was told that the student had been moved to "a more loving teacher." I stepped into the principal's office to request a meeting and was told, "Herbert's dad apologizes for his profanity towards you, but he wants you to understand that he and his wife worked too hard on that report for you to fail their son. I want you to reconsider changing his grade. After all, he was trying on the draft." I declined. He responded with, "I want kids to love coming here. If they don't want to write, *stop forcing them!* Stop cramming it down their throat! Keeping parents happy keeps our school functioning. We love our students, we *don't* fail them."

I did not change that grade. I did not lose my dignity. My only sadness is that Herbert is going to be a non-productive member of society in seven years. Maybe by the time his parents need assisted living, he will have learned to put down the video game controller long enough to wipe his own butt and will have made a few friends on Fortnite who will take care of him.

IT'S ANNOYING

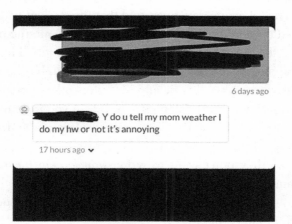

6 days ago

Y do u tell my mom weather I do my hw or not it's annoying

17 hours ago

A SUDDEN REALIZATION

ANONYMOUS

Last year I was pregnant with my first child and so excited to tell my students. I teach middle school ESL, and I have six different classes. All day long I announced my news and it was met with cheers and congratulations. It was finally my last class of the day, and I told my seventh grade students the news. One boy in the class very quietly raised his hand and I thought he would have a question about my due date or if I knew if it was a boy or a girl. When I called on him, he very loudly said, "Miss! So that means you fuck!" Seconds later the fire alarm went off for a fire drill and he bolted out of the door before I could even address the issue. I was left mouth agape and utterly shocked. When we returned from the drill, I sent him to the office for administration to deal with. The student never received any consequence nor did he apologize for what he said.

BUT DID YOU DIE?

J. MORRIS

Recently, I started a conversation online about how insensitive some administrators can be when it comes to teachers being ill. I was genuinely surprised at how many teachers have experienced this. Besides the fact that it's illegal to ask an employee for any details about their illness, it is also unlawful to prevent them from taking leave if they or a family member are ill. But these admins don't flat-out tell you not to take leave. Instead, they make you feel really bad about it. Just look at the following examples:

"A year ago I was on life support. The day after I got off of it, my principal sent me a text asking when my report cards would be finished."

"I had a giant kid step on my foot and ankle. It swelled up instantly and turned black and purple. The principal was annoyed that I had to go to an urgent care to get an X-ray and asked me what I could have done to prevent it."

"My doctor told me in late October that I was seriously sick and needed surgery right then. I told my principal, who informed me that one time he had a cracked molar, and he had to wait until summer to fix it. I worked until winter break and had renal failure afterward because I waited so long."

"When my son was six, he required surgery and was put on life support. I got a call from my principal. I thought he was going to ask me how my son was doing. Instead, he told me that I was declared surplus and should start looking at listings so I could apply for another job!"

"I had an extremely high-risk pregnancy, during which I had to go for ultrasounds downtown every Friday. The principal had the audacity to say to me, 'You're taking off another Friday? Can't you do it another day or on the weekend?' BITCH! As if I *want* to be going to potentially find out something else is wrong with my unborn child."

"One of my children was in the hospital in an oxygen tent and struggling to breathe. My principal asked if I could find someone else to sit with her while I came to work."

"My school made me get written proof from the funeral home that I was actually at my grandma's funeral."

"My house burned down one night. Thankfully we all got out safely, but I had to figure out where we were going to live and what we were going to do. We had absolutely nothing. I returned to school two weeks later, and my principal threatened my job, scolded me for 'carelessly handing my class over to my co-teacher,' and made fun of me for having a panic attack during a fire drill."

"I was hospitalized for a high fever, and we quickly found out I was septic and in danger of dying. My vice-principal called me and said she was worried that I might not get my report card grades finished on time. I had to input grades from my hospital bed."

"I had an ectopic pregnancy that, thankfully, was caught very early. I was lucky that medical intervention would prevent the need for surgery. I had no sick leave left, so I had to work through the excruciating pain and messy expulsion. I left the profession after that."

"I had emergency brain surgery and legitimately almost died. My principal was pissed because grades were due. My husband had to spend hours on the phone with several teachers and administrators to walk them through how to find my grades online. Four months later, my principal asked me how my surgery went. I left teaching soon after."

"My wife's water broke six weeks early on the first day of school. Many parents told me off for missing the first day, even though my son was in the NICU."

"I landed in the hospital once after a deadly allergic reaction to penicillin. I sent the principal a message that I was going to be out the next day, and I had already secured a sub. His response was, 'Don't let this happen again during testing week.' Okay, I'll just die at work next time."

"My daughter was diagnosed with childhood cancer. After a month of being out, they kicked me out of my classroom and told me I could either be a substitute teacher, teach only kids who had been expelled from school, or resign. Later on, they realized that what they had done was against the law, so I got to resign with full pay and benefits."

"My principal told me that we needed to have a serious meeting because I missed a testing day due to having a miscarriage. I was in severe pain, deep depression, and utterly heartbroken while I got scolded for having missed a day of work. My doctor told me I should go on leave because my anemia was really bad and I was blacking out a lot, but I kept working because I was afraid I would get in trouble again."

"I was struggling with infertility and managed to get an appointment with a top-rated fertility doctor. I needed to leave school one hour early. When I told my principal the situation, she rolled her eyes, told me she'd have to think about whether or not she would let me leave early and called my classroom a few hours later to say, 'You should be really grateful that I am allowing you to leave early.'"

"My husband is an assistant principal, and when you work in the same district as your spouse, you can use each other's unused sick days. The only problem is that you need the principal's permission. I had a very high-risk pregnancy, and my doctor sent the principal a note explaining that 'high-risk twins at 38-years-old is catastrophic to the patient's health and can be potentially fatal to that of the babies.' He denied the request for my husband's sick days multiple times, stating, 'Pregnancy is not catastrophic.' His statement was supported by the teachers' union."

"My grandmother was dying, and I wanted to take a trip across the country to say goodbye. I was told by an administrator that they couldn't prevent me from going but that it would be a terrible idea to leave during state testing (for third graders). I had to say goodbye to her over the phone, and it is one of my biggest regrets."

"My principal asked to see my bruises after I was in a head-on collision. I had only missed two days of school but spent three years dealing with concussion-related issues because I didn't listen to my doctor and stay home to rest."

"My husband was dying of cancer, and my principal wanted me to provide a doctor's note when I tried to take one day off to be with him on our last wedding anniversary."

"I had an administrator who was angry that I missed the Harvest Festival because I was 400 miles away at my sister's funeral."

"When I told the principal I was pregnant with my third child, he said, 'Is this going to keep happening?'"

CAUTION: UNSTABLE PARENT BEHIND THE WHEEL

ANONYMOUS

I WORKED AT A PRIVATE MIDDLE SCHOOL WITH VERY competitive parents. They had extremely high expectations for their kids and were often unrealistic in their expectations of the teachers (and perception of what their kids were capable of). A parent set up a private meeting with me to discuss the 8 out of 10 that his son received on a spelling quiz. The parent had an entire argument written out for why the grading was unfair, and that the points should be given back. A spelling test is pretty straightforward, so I just reiterated that his son spelled two words wrong, which lost him two points. He responded with, "He is young. These are minor mistakes. He does not deserve a B." I continued to explain that an 8 out of 10 is a B and that if I gave him the points back, it would be unfair to the other students. The parent stormed out of the meeting and slammed the door.

A few days later, the same parent was dropping off his son and saw me crossing the street. He waited and then *purposefully* ran me over. We looked right into each other's eyes as he did it. It was 100% on purpose. The security guard saw the whole incident and helped me into the building as the parent sped away.

I felt okay at first but had terrible pains later in the day and went to the hospital. I experienced severely herniated discs and had to have three separate surgeries, but the pain never completely went away. I still take pain meds every day and attend bi-weekly physical therapy.

I was afraid to press charges against the parent because he was unstable, and I feared for myself and my children. I did take him to civil court to win damages for my injuries. I won the case but have not seen a penny from that parent, and the only recourse I have is for him to be jailed for not paying, which I won't do, as I explained earlier.

Meanwhile, the administration at my school has been entirely unsupportive. They knew all of the events that had happened and had numerous doctors' reports but refused to renew my contract at the end of the year for my excessive absences and said that I was "uncooperative." I also received a letter from the state that because of the amount of time I was out, I would need to take several courses to renew my teaching license.

I won't be doing that. After everything I have been through, I consider it impossible for me to enter a classroom ever again.

PHANTOM POOPERS ACROSS THE NATION

J. MORRIS

I ASKED MY TEACHER FOLLOWERS TO TELL ME THE strangest locations they have found poop in their school. I specified that these should be mainstream K-12 stories (in case you are wondering if there is a reasonable explanation for these.) I received over one thousand responses.

Locations include: the nozzle of a hand dryer; on a lunch plate in the cafeteria; in a homework turn-in tray; in a shoebox with the lid on it; in the stapler and stapled to the bulletin board; on the principal's chair, desk and door, in other kids' lunch boxes; in another kid's winter boots; smeared on the door handle; in other kids' jacket pockets; in a hat that his friend then put on; in the radiator during winter; spread on a handrail; in a poster tube; in a teacher's filing cabinet; on the dance floor after a school dance; in a Valentine's day card left in the hallway; all over a standardized test; on top of a skylight; inside a printer; on top of a dollar bill; inside the fluorescent light cover; in a trophy case; in the coin slot of a vending machine; on a plastic hall pass; inside a pencil case; in a cubby; in a fish tank; hanging from a coat hook; in a kid's own shirt pocket; in a teacher's briefcase; in other kids' backpacks; under a hat left on the floor; on the bathroom ceiling; on the computer lab walls and smeared into the keyboards; on the rafters above the stage; on the roof of a portable classroom; in a potted plant; under or in a teacher's desk; in a Fritos bag in the gym; in a locker; in the recycling bin; in a tuba; in an instrument case; and on a wrestling mat. The most frequent locations to find poop are the water fountains, bathroom sinks, urinals, soap dispensers, reading carpets and stairwells.

I don't know what's up with kids and poop. I don't recall ever feeling inclined to leave my poop anywhere in the school. I wouldn't even consider actually pooping in the toilets at school.

SPIRITUAL ACTIVITY

ANONYMOUS

I HAD A CHALLENGING, MISBEHAVED STUDENT. SINCE the day I met him, his mother made excuses for his behavior, such as, "He doesn't act this way at home," or "He watches the older kids in the neighborhood act this way." He was often unkind with his words and hit his classmates, despite being spoken to many times.

One week, in particular, he was exceptionally harsh to his classmates, and it needed to be addressed immediately. I asked to speak with his mother after school. I was prepared for an excuse when I told her about his behavior, but I was not ready for the excuse she gave me. She said, "Oh, I know exactly why he is behaving like this. We have spiritual activity in our house, and he is frightened!"

"Oh? Can you tell me more about that?" I responded. She said, "Our dog barks at absolutely everything, and I mean *everything*. Suddenly, he no longer barks! He is quiet all the time! Plus, I went to put his clothes away, and there was a shirt on the floor! I *know* that my son didn't put it there!"

"Wow, sounds scary!" I said. "But be that as it may, he

cannot push his friends off the slide or call them mean names." I was dumbfounded.

"I am getting our house blessed this weekend," she said. "Let me know if his behavior is any better next week."

His behavior did not improve after the house blessing, so I guess the spiritual activity continued...

A HORRIBLE, INACCURATE GIFT

To: School Counselor
From: Zorak's mother
Subject: Inaccurate grade

I just checked Zorak's grades online and they are horrible. There is no way this is accurate. Either the information on the school's website is inaccurate or no one is updating the information which is why it is inaccurate. I know it is Christmas day but I would like a response as soon as possible because these grades were like a horrible gift I opened today. I am seriously considering switching schools.

IT TAKES A MACHETE
ANONYMOUS

I am a Health and Phys. Ed. teacher and a student gave me a concussion on purpose.

I told one of the assistant principals that a male student was skipping class. I then went to my next class and took the students outside to the track. During this time, the student I had told on was scolded by the assistant principal. He was angry and came looking for me. He saw I was out near the track, grabbed a soccer ball, and took it outside. He quietly walked up behind me and kicked it as hard as he could, hitting me in the lower back of my head. I jolted forward, completely stunned, and heard him laughing hysterically. A girl who was sitting with me said, "I saw the whole thing, and it was definitely on purpose."

I took her to the assistant principal, and we both explained what had happened. The kid only got one day out-of-school suspension, and I was told I couldn't prove intent, despite the girl's testimony! I was out of work from the beginning of October until I came back in late April, but only part-time. When I returned, I asked the principal to please keep the student who attacked me out of my classes but I was told that his infractions weren't that bad, and that I was paranoid. I started to wonder, *"What does it take for a student to get a true consequence around here?"*

A month later, the student was expelled because he brought a machete to school while also having drugs on him. No one apologized to me or acknowledged what he had done.

YOU HATE OUR SCHOOL? PUBLICLY LYING ABOUT IT WILL HELP!

To: School staff
From: Principal
Subject: New checkout requirement

Dear staff,
Since staff morale has been so low lately, we have added one last task for you to complete before you sign out for the summer. Please leave a minimum of two positive reviews of our school somewhere on the internet (Google, Yelp, Niche) and print them to verify with me before checkout. I am hoping this process helps you focus on what makes our school great and renews an appreciation for this wonderful place before we break for the summer. See me with questions.

MEANINGFUL FEEDBACK

J. MORRIS

WHEN AN ADULT DOESN'T LIKE THEIR SERVICE AT A restaurant, they can express themselves on Yelp. When they get poor care at a doctor's office, they can review their experience on ZocDoc. Until 2019, kids had a very public online forum to express their dissatisfaction with their teachers on a site called Ratemyteachers.com. This very popular site allowed anyone in the world to look up a teacher by name or by school, and see what people had posted anonymously about them. It not only rated their performance, but it rated their popularity as well. It was a very irritating thing for a lot of teachers. Kids could write pretty much anything they wanted about their teacher, and it could be found by merely googling the teacher's name. The worst comment I received during my first year of teaching was that I had no control of the class, and it was true for that one very challenging class. However, fifteen years later, I definitely don't want people judging me based on a comment from my first year of teaching. But that comment was nothing compared to some that other teachers received. Here are some of the most humorous comments I saw:

"He makes me want to jump off something tall and land on something sharp. I have a theory that he harvests the tears of his students so that he can drink them and have eternal life. I have never seen a better looking human-ptero-dactyl hybrid."

"Although this man is a terrific trombone player, he is a terrible person, and I hate him."

"He reminds me of a disgruntled shopping mall Santa."

"I honestly think I could wake up with swine flu, and my left nut alone could still be a better professor."

"All the allure of a pepperoni induced burp."

"Hates the constitution. Smells like a wet dog who got sprayed by a skunk. Someone should discuss hygiene with her. A bar of soap and a toothbrush isn't too much to ask."

"Has the personality of a sea-slug."

"I don't wear my seatbelt when driving to school because I want to die before I can make it to this class."

"The only thing interesting about him is his fanny pack."

Ratemyteachers.com got so many complaints to the Better Business Bureau about the comments being racist, homophobic, sexist, and threatening that they completely changed their approach. Teachers everywhere breathed a sigh of relief when they learned that the site was purchased from its original owner in 2018, and all of the initial comments were deleted! You can still leave comments, but the site claims it will remove anything "inappropriate, libelous, defamatory, indecent, vulgar or obscene, porno-graphic, sexually explicit or sexually suggestive, racially, culturally, or ethnically offensive, harmful, harassing, intimidating, threatening, hateful, objectionable, discriminatory, or abusive." If the site gets as popular as it used to be, I don't know how they will keep up with vetting all those comments.

Until 2018, Ratemyprofessors.com actually gave the option to rate a teacher's "hotness." If the teacher got enough votes, they got a hot tamale icon next to their name. After a professor tweeted that this tamale was utterly irrelevant and often sexist, her comment went viral, and the site removed the "hotness" rating option. But the site still gives anyone the chance to comment about a professor with absolutely no filter, anonymously. Here are some totally irrelevant, and insulting comments you can read on the site:

"She looks like a meerkat."

"Your lipstick is too dark."

"Doesn't care how students think the class should be run. Her attitude is like, I'm the teacher, so it's my decision."

"Unhelpful. All he did was tell me to meet him during lunch or before or after school, and told me how to get tutoring."

"I don't think she's human."

"You're like a badass leprechaun."

"You should wear more makeup."

"Looks like Jabba the Hutt."

"TOTAL BITCH."

"I can tell by your shoes that you have a puppy."

"Total ball buster. I think it's cuz she's so short."

"Acts like he knows more than we do."

"Dat ass doe."

"He's my homie."

"Her voice is so annoying I wanted to kill someone."

"All you talk about is books. Talk about something else."

"I don't think she wears a bra. If she does, she needs a better one."

"You suck at teaching and life I think."

"She was probably pretty hot when she was in high school."

"Her hair is dumb."

"You have to ask for help, he won't just help you."

"He is bae."

"Doesn't let you sleep in class."

"Stop using big words."

"He's like a black unicorn."

"He looks like a Lego."

"Undoubtedly spawned from the womb of Satan."

"Always has a face like a bulldog licking an electric fence."

"Looks like a gnome."

"Fire AF."

"Not a bad teacher, just a bad person."

"Total demon."

"Looks like Bert from Sesame Street."

"Worse than a rabid dog that bit me."

"Smells like old Band-Aids."

"She's too old."

"I want to throw stuff at her."

"If you have a choice between going to this class and being covered in gravy and locked in a room with a wolverine that is high on bath salts, pick the wolverine."

"Won't let you eat anything, play on your phone or sleep. Worst class. Worst teacher."

"She looks like someone threw a Barbie doll in a fryer."

"I think he's a butt pirate."

"Ruined my life."

"Your skirts are too long."

"Never taught anything, just spent the whole time explaining stuff."

"Your beard is majestic and it looks like it could nurture a nest of baby birds."

"I think you should try to part your hair on the other side."

"She's a train wreck."

"She forced us to be respectful to everyone and it was very annoying."

"Give us food."

"Nutin cuh we good."

I think it's obvious that a lot of students are not mature enough to handle rating their teacher's class. Yet still, many secondary teachers and almost all college professors are forced to give their students evaluation forms to complete. The teacher's reputation and job security often rest heavily on this feedback. Perhaps that needs to change, or nah?

PURPOSEFUL PEASANTS

We are in full-refresh mode of refining and
practicing *purposeful presence.* You have heard it
before, know it and do it often! Let's refine our
practice and provide each other feedback in order
to reach our goal of being *100% purposefully
present* at all times during the school day when we
are with students.

Purposeful presence:
- **Hands free** (ex. no coffee (!), phones,
  computers)
- **Strong, intentional stance** (ex. standing not
  sitting or leaning, facing students)
- **Purposeful acknowledgment of students**
  (ex. good morning, redirection)

This morning during arrival purposeful presence
was observed in **9/13** samples = **69%** of the
time.

BUS DRIVER TELLS KIDS TO GO FUCK THEMSELVES

J. MORRIS

THE FOLLOWING IS A ROUNDUP OF NEWS HEADLINES from 2019:

- School Administrator Accused of Showing up Drunk to School during Alcohol Awareness Week
- Middle School Student Charged with Attempting to Poison Teacher
- Ohio Teacher Resigns for Taping Students' Mouths Shut
- Driver Tells Kids to 'Go Fuck Themselves' and Then Abandons School Bus at Gas Station
- Teen Arrested for Attempting Wrestling Move on High School Principal, Police Say
- Teacher Accused of Threatening to Cut off Student's Penis during Kickball Game
- Louisiana Students Laced Teacher's Drink with Cleaning Solution, Filmed it on Snapchat
- Students Overdosing, Active Shooter Drills and Buying Supplies with his Own Salary: Teacher

Quits after 20 years and Reveals Why the
'Toxic' Profession has Made Him Leave

- Police: Eighth Grader Stabs Rutherford
  Principal with Folding Knife at Graduation
  Practice
- Substitute Teacher Fired for Filming Porn in
  Classroom
- Art Teacher Accused of Stealing Craft Supplies
  from Walmart
- Prank Sent Teacher to Hospital Fighting for
  Her Life after Allergic Reaction
- City Teachers Flood Sugar-Daddy Site for
  Extra Income
- Mom Upset with Re-zoning, Threatens
  Shooting at Barton Elementary School
- Police: Cobb Student Punched Teacher Who
  Asked About Assignment
- No Teacher's Strike as District Says it's Got
  More Money than it thought it Did
- Richardson ISD Student Allegedly Uses Taser
  on High School Staff Member
- The Day Maggots Fell from the Ceiling: Why I
  Quit Teaching
- Substitute Teacher Arrested for Downing 4
  Vodka Shots during Class
- Student Arrested for Threatening to Shoot Up
  School Because He Couldn't Smoke a Joint
- Teacher Left in Tears after Principal
  Confiscates Pizzas She Bought for
  Hardworking Students because 'it wasn't fair to
  other classes'

Here are some nice ones, just to keep things balanced:

- Nine-Year-Old Saves Cousin Choking On Lifesaver by Performing Lifesaving Heimlich
- High School Robotics Team Makes Sweet Rides for Kids with Disabilities
- Four-Year-Old Raises Over $50K for Homeless Vets after Asking a Good Question: "If they're Heroes, Why Should They be on the Street?"
- High School Students Build New Arm for Disabled Girl So She Can Be a Bionic Cello Player
- Teen Launches Nonprofit To Throw Birthday Parties for Homeless Kids
- Classmates of Third Grader Who Lost Everything in a Fire Surprise Him with a 'Secret Toy Drive'
- Teacher's Shoes were Stolen from His Classroom, so His Students Surprised Him with New Ones
- High School Lets Students Replace P.E. With Volunteer Yard Work for Elderly and Disabled People
- Generous 9-Year-Old Saved Allowance to Pay off His Entire Class's Lunch Debt
- Heroic High Schoolers Rush To Help Senior Hit By Out-Of-Control Car
- 30-Year-Old Man with Special Needs and Nowhere to Go Gets Taken In By His Former Teacher, Given His First Birthday Party
- Boy Bullied For Homemade Shirt Raises Almost $1M for Anti-Bullying Nonprofit
- First Graders Persuaded School to Adopt

Therapy Dog—and Their Story Won $100K for Shelter That Housed Him

- 10-Year-Old Has Been Donating Hundreds of Pajamas and Books for Children Spending the Holidays in Shelters
- Kids Are Hailed as 'Junior Detectives' after they Successfully Track Down Missing 97-Year-Old with Dementia
- Instead of Using Birthday Money for Disney World Vacation, 6-Year-Old Uses It to Feed Hurricane Evacuees

I DID NOT LIKE IT

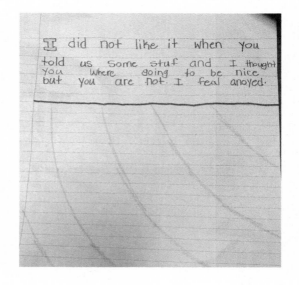

GET ON THAT SKYPE!

ALEXA, PITTSBURGH, PENNSYLVANIA

I'M AN ELEMENTARY SCHOOL TEACHER, AND I HAD A personal day scheduled, so a substitute was called in. The morning after my day off, the sub came to me in tears, saying the kids were so bad and disrespectful she would not cover my class ever again. I shared this information with my administration, hoping they'd understand and offer help for the next time I was out. Instead, the principals (we have four of them for a building of K-5 students) insisted that when I am out, I Skype into the class to assist with classroom management.

Yes, you heard me right! Skype in on my personal days to be sure the 10-year-olds don't act like assholes when we have four principals, two guidance counselors, a student support specialist, and an entire mental health unit at my school! I nodded with the, "Yeah, okay" look and mouthed, "Get the fuck outta here" as I left the office.

DEMON BOOK SELECTION

From: Vanjie's mother
Subject: Urgent! Haunted book

Hello,
I really need your help. The book that Vanjie
bought at the book fair is causing a huge
problem in our house. I told her that she needs
to take it back and exchange it for something
else immediately. She told me that you said
there are no refunds and nothing to exchange it
for, since the book fair is over. We cannot have
the book in our home. I know that it says it is
for a kid her age, but we have already had to
deal with 7 demons in our home. This would be
opening the door for another. I need to know
what to do about this.

TOILET SEATS AND OTHER CREATIVE HALL PASSES

J. MORRIS

A LOT OF SCHOOLS WILL ALLOW TEACHERS TO CHOOSE their own object to give to students to use as a hall pass. Some will go the standard root with a laminated card or a lanyard. But others take this as an opportunity to embarrass their students and have some fun.

Real hall passes teachers have used:

- An actual toilet seat (*Just in case you need an extra*)
- A mannequin leg (*Cuz why not?*)
- A rotting plantain (*Can't let that go to waste!*)
- A giant cinder block (*Though it was confiscated by admin because it could be used as a weapon*)
- A sign that says "I have explosive diarrhea" (*How badly do you have to go, kid?*)
- A rubber rat on a leash (*Because it's a funny image to see a kid walking a rat on a leash*

*through the hallways and teachers are desperate
for laughs)*

- A sign that just says "poop" on it (*Short and to
the point.*)
- A screwdriver (*This seems like a bad idea to me.
See the earlier note about the cinder block being
used as a weapon*)
- A toaster (*In case anyone needs to make toast in
the bathroom.*)
- An old bowling pin (*Cuz why not?*)
- A giant cardboard cutout of Burt Reynolds'
head (*Cuz Burt Reynolds.*)
- Giant cardboard cutout of Britney Spears (*She
wants to watch you pee.*)
- An upright bass (*Cuz why not?*)
- A huge hazard cone (*Perhaps you might need to
put it in the doorway after you go?*)
- A fake Christmas tree (*Are you feeling festive?*)
- A red cape the student must wear that says,
"Pee, poop & away!" (*Public humiliation in
exchange for using the restroom.*)
- A huge, old, heavy computer monitor (*Just so
you appreciate modern tech.*)
- A baby car seat (*They're heavier than they look.
Think long and hard about that while you pee.*)
- A huge jar of dirt (*Cuz why not?*)
- A creepy old naked baby doll (*It wants to
creepily watch you pee.*)
- A creepy old baby doll head (*It wants to creepily
watch you pee.*)
- An oar (*In case there is a sudden and massive
flood in the bathroom!*)

- A life jacket (*In case there is a sudden and massive flood in the bathroom!*)
- A surfboard (*In case there is a sudden and massive flood in the bathroom!*)
- A gigantic cardboard cutout of the teacher's head (*There is no way I would let an image of myself go into the student bathroom.*)
- A baby stroller (*Cuz why not?*)
- An iron block (*In case you need to defend yourself.*)
- A huge bottle of hand sanitizer (*Great idea. Just make sure you sanitize the sanitizer!*)
- A cactus (*Cuz why not?*)
- A bicycle wheel (*Cuz why not?*)
- A skeleton foot (*Creepy yet inventive.*)
- A mop with the wheelie bucket of soap and everything (*Go to the bathroom, and while you're in there, clean the place up!*)
- A 5 foot long, 40 pound block of wood with "Hall Pass" carved into it (*Are you strong enough to use the bathroom?*)
- A toilet plunger (*In case you clog that shit up!*)
- A laminated poster of Cardi B but it says, "Cardi Pee" on it (*Clever and amusing!*)
- A large wooden crab that says, "I've got crabs" (*Public humiliation in exchange for using the restroom.*)

JUST STAY IN YOUR LANE

ANONYMOUS

I was very excited to become a teacher. I was especially happy to work at the middle school I went to, that my daughter was also attending. Before the school year even started, I was pulled into the principal's office (a man I've known for over 20 years now) for two separate "infractions:" yelling at my daughter in the hall (I was trying to get her attention to tell her where to meet me after school), and attempting to ask *one* question during the staff meeting earlier that day. I was told that I should not ask questions in meetings, so I'm not deemed "annoying," and I shouldn't shout at my child in public, especially when we had parents and incoming students touring the building. He specifically said, "You are a first-year teacher, so you have a target on your back. You need to fit in, or you won't be teaching here next year."

A month or so later, I was called to his office in the middle of class. I walked in, and my department head, the principal, and an assistant principal were waiting in the office. I was told that there had been some complaints that I was "too helpful" and that I need to learn to stay in my lane and not help others. I was also told that it's great that I'm so passionate about my job, but my passion is being seen as annoying. Again, I was told to fit in, or I wouldn't have a job at the end of the year.

Cut to late October when I was asked to come in for yet another meeting where I was told that I need to be put on a Growth Plan. No one had observed my classes or anything like that. The principal said that my expectations were too high, and students felt like giving up because of that. When I asked for specifics of what expectations were too high and which students wanted to give up, he didn't answer. He just said that a teacher overheard me say, "I hate all of you equally," which was a running joke in my class, and definitely meant in a lighthearted way. The teacher even told the principal that she did not hear what I had said before or after that. Another teacher claimed I pulled into the parking lot too fast, which obviously had nothing to do with my teaching.

The Growth Plan was simply for me to read a specific teaching book and write summaries on each chapter. The plan was supposed to be completed by February 1st, with growth being shown via observations. In that time, they observed me once.

A couple of weeks later, the principal stormed into my classroom in the middle of class and said that I'm on a power trip about phones, because I confiscated a student's phone, as per the school's phone policy. He then said, "Just stay in your lane! I think we just need to get through this year and be done with it!"

In January, I was called in for a conference. I had been assuming that my contract would not be renewed, but since things had been going really well, and I finished the summaries early, I figured maybe I had a chance. He said that he met with HR about the upcoming year, and he recommended my contract not be extended due to how many times he had met with me about growth. This man never once attempted to talk to me about how I was doing, never observed my classes, and my Growth Plan wasn't even over at that time. He said, "You have shown growth, but it is not enough to stay here. I will give you a good recommendation unless something goes sideways before the end of the school year." Then I was expected to finish the rest of the year knowing I wouldn't have a job anymore.

AN OMINOUS MESSAGE FROM YOUR PRINCIPAL

To: Staff
From: Principal
Subject: Beware

I wonder how many untruths are out there and how many of us are acting or feeling based on something that never occurred. Please be careful of wolves in sheep's clothing and watch the cunning ways of those who seem to seek confusion. Often they are the sole author of it all and until the light is shining brightly upon them, they will leave a trail of devastation in their path.

Don't forget we have a faculty meeting tomorrow and book study is Friday. Have a great evening!

IMAGINARY FRIEND

ANONYMOUS

My FIRST YEAR OF TEACHING WAS AT A STARTUP charter school in a rough neighborhood. I taught third grade. They accepted anyone who got expelled from public school for behavioral issues.

One kid had an imaginary friend that he would continuously talk to under his breath. It was extremely frightening. One day while taking attendance, I heard him scream out, "Help me!" I looked up, and literally, no one was touching him or even near him. He stood up, backed up against the wall, and started acting like someone was strangling him. It dawned on the entire class and me that it was his imaginary friend who was attacking him.

I pushed the code red button and stood by the door. I was definitely not getting in the middle of his fight with his imaginary friend. While I waited for help, I tried to make sure the kids who were dying from laughter were staying seated. One student stood on top of his desk and yelled out, "I'll fuck up your imaginary friend!" He was punching the air and screaming out curse words, trying to beat up the imaginary friend.

The student who was in distress seemed to calm down a bit in response to this, so I thought I would help too. While standing by the doorway, I began to tell the imaginary friend to leave. I yelled out that he is not a student at the school, and he is not welcome here. A bunch of the other students started helping me by screaming, "Get the hell out of our class!" and throwing fists and kicks. Although it was weird as hell, it was actually kind of a nice bonding moment for our class. We all banded together to help the student get rid of his abusive imaginary friend.

But that's the moment that administration walked in. They saw me, the teacher, yelling at no one. One student was standing on the desk, punching the air and screaming, "Fuck you!" while the rest screamed and made a racket. The student in the back was rolling around on the ground while his imaginary friend strangled him. Admin took him out of the room and called his mom to pick him up. I urged his mom to take him for a psychological evaluation. He was never given an evaluation by the school and he never received help. They just told me that what they saw in my room, they "never want to see again."

DON'T TELL MY DAUGHTER I'M AN ASSHOLE!

Hi Mrs. ▪▪▪ this is ▪▪▪'s mom and I would like to ask you if ▪▪▪ could get an extra assignment to lift up her science grade. I feel that my daughter is getting academically distracted due to her doing YOUR job, in helping out one of YOUR students, and I feel like you are not giving my daughter an opportunity to raise her grades, so she can have straight A's, and also, you are not fulfilling your duties as a teacher, in assisting my daughter, when she needed your help, specifically during the persuasive essay. Due to you not helping her out, when she needed your assistance, she turned in her assignment late, and not only did you not help her on time, you took away points due to your wrong doing. And I would like for my daughter to not know about this email, incase you want to contact me for further conversation, my number is ▪▪▪ Thanks for your time.

MY EYEBROWS HURT AND OTHER MEDICAL EMERGENCIES

J. MORRIS

I RECENTLY FOUND OUT THAT MANY SCHOOLS DO NOT have a nurse or medical professional on the premises. At first, this seemed terrible. But when I asked a few school nurses for their favorite excuses that students give for visiting their office, I see that most of their time is probably spent telling kids they are fine, explaining to them that their supposed illnesses or ailments are not actually possible, and sending them back to class. It's funny that teachers even allow them to leave class for these reasons, but you know they just need a break from the kid who has an itchy tooth.

Here are the best reasons for which students have visited the school nurse:

(*written on pass by teacher*) "Sucking on arm. Left a mark."

"I fell in the toilet."

(*written on pass by teacher*) "Pringle in eye."

"I ate a rock."

(*written on pass by teacher*) "Complains of headache whenever we sing Jingle Bells."

"My feet itch."

(*written on pass by teacher*) "Eye hurts from homemade arrow that hit eye one year ago."

"My eyebrows hurt."

(*written on pass by teacher*) "Tight pants."

"I almost sneezed."

"I don't know why I'm here. My teacher just sent me."

"My poop is like water!"

"I had a sharp, sideways poop."

"My tooth is itchy."

(*written on pass by teacher*) "Ate cupcake wrapper."

"I popped a pimple in my ear."

"My shoes are too big."

"I think I need my arm amputated."

(*written on pass by teacher*) "Ate a snail."

"I have to fart."

(*written on pass by teacher*) "Student's mom sent essential oils to rub on moles on student's back."
(*Nurse's response*) "Sorry, but unless the oil came with a doctor's note I am not allowed to administer it."

(*written on pass by teacher*) "Sweater stuck in braces."

"I looked at the sun at recess, and I keep seeing spots."

(*written on pass by teacher*) "Hand glued shut."

"Do you have any pregnancy tests?"

"I'm sick because my friend threw up on the bus."

"I have a headache because I was swimming yesterday and someone peed in the pool."

"I think there's a hair in my mouth."

"My dog has worms. I think I have them too. I feel them in my eyes."

"I got yogurt in my shoe."

"I farted and it smelled really bad."

(*written on pass by teacher*) "Needs ointment."
Nurse: "What do you need ointment for?"
Student: "I don't know."

Student: "I can't see the board so my teacher sent me here to tell you."
Nurse: "How long have you had trouble seeing the board?"
Student: "Just today."
Nurse: "Only today? Why do you think that is?"
Student: "My friend was sitting in front of me and he's tall."

Student: "When I bend my arm like this it hurts."
Nurse: "Don't bend your arm like that."
Student: "Okay."

And here are some unbelievably specific absence excuses:

"Her pet llama died."
"Had to milk the goats."
"My mom had her period and wouldn't drive me to school."
"My calves were sore."
"My daughter was out yesterday because it was too windy."
"My son will be out this week. He was involved in a small incident and cannot wear shoes."
"We had a birthday party for my cat."
"I won't be into school today because I'm relaxing in the hot tub after a long skiing weekend."
"She will be attending her rat's funeral."
"My grandma saw a ghost so I couldn't come to school."
"Our dog has fleas."
"There was an earthquake and my mom and dad fell

through the ground and I had to pull them out and I broke my arm." (*No visible cast.*)

"There were ants in the kitchen."

"I went to a Groundhog's Day celebration."

"My goat's teat exploded in the middle of the night."

95

BECAUSE, YA KNOW, BUTTHOLES

ANONYMOUS

I'M A KINDERGARTEN TEACHER. MOST OF THE TIME, I enjoy the kids. I'm high energy and goofy, and so are they. We match perfectly. Last year, however, was a year straight from hell.

You know those kids who were never on your roster until the first day of school because their parents never cared to enroll them on time? Yeah, I got a few of those. One boy who I will call "Pork Chop" was difficult due to a behavioral diagnosis, so it was not entirely his fault, although he had never been given a boundary in his life. He was influenced by the beast we will call "Jiggly."

Jiggly was something else. She bit, hissed, slobbered ugly crying, smacked people, and even ate an orange with the peel on. Needless to say, Jiggly had never been to preschool or really ever socialized outside of her house. *Ever.* This is how you create nightmarish children.

One day, during their insane daily antics, I noticed Pork Chop and Jiggly under a table, somewhat disguised by chairs. I walk over to tell them to please come back to the carpet. When I bent down, I saw Jiggly's pants down, and

179

she was on all fours. Her butthole was directed straight at Pork Chop's face. I'm talking eleven inches away maximum. Did this smell pleasant? No way in hell. Jiggly didn't bathe very often, that's for sure.

Meanwhile, Pork Chop was giggling and seemingly enjoying the butthole being so close to his face. Jiggly was laughing as well, because, ya know, *buttholes*. As I started to yell at her for being inappropriate, I saw Pork Chop's finger slowly raise into the air. I still remember that the whole situation began to feel like it was moving in slow motion as I yelled, "*Nooooooo!*"

But it was too late.

His finger entered her butthole as her laughing increased tenfold. I shrieked, which made them stop immediately. It was as though they didn't really know that what they were doing was utterly horrifying. I screamed, "Get up!" about fifty times as they climbed out from under the desks, and Jiggly pulled her pants back up.

I ran across the hall to vent to my friends, all while trying not to vomit. When I came back into the classroom, both kids were smelling Pork Chop's finger and laughing hysterically. I didn't speak directly to them for days as I tried to process what had happened. I was too embarrassed to report it to administration because I didn't want to go over what had happened ever again. I also knew they wouldn't do anything about it, and somehow I would be blamed.

And that is one small episode of what was just another day in my kindergarten classroom.

ASKING TOO MUCH

To: Social Studies Teacher
From: Silky's mother
Subject: Need help

Dear Mr. Davenport,
My daughter Silky started her period a few
months ago and is very shy about it. She's so
shy that she doesn't want to change her pad at
school because she thinks someone will know
she has her period. I'm afraid that she might
smell down there. Do you think you could find a
way, without embarrassing her, to smell down
there and if there is any odor just quietly
remind her to change her pad?

HOW TO KILL IMAGINARY CHICKENS

LIZ CARLSON (@SHELOVESTEACHINGFOURTH), ALBERTA,
CANADA

SEVERAL YEARS AGO, A GOOD FRIEND AND I WERE teaching fourth grade. We each had interesting students that year with similar attributes. I had one who thought he was a dog. He literally walked on all fours, barked, panted, growled, scratched behind his ears, and refused to be called by his real name. He wished to be called Bingo, his dog's name.

My teaching assistant and I made the mistake of answering him when he asked what our dogs' names were. He started to call me Timber and her Sasha. He addressed the other students by their dogs' names as well (Oreo, Max, Daisy, etc.). This behavior was going to have to change, and the sooner, the better.

By the end of the first month, we had persuaded him that he could not engage in any dog-like behavior in class or call anyone by dog names. However, the deal we made with him was that if he behaved like a human in class, he could be a dog as much as he wanted during recess. For the entire year, and I mean *the entire school year*, he crawled around on the playground on all fours, regardless of the weather (and I taught in Canada, where our school was built on swampland.) He would often come back inside soaked with mud, but didn't seem to care.

The following year he entered fifth grade, which means he started middle school. He had completely dropped the dog routine but became extremely obsessed with The Mamas and The Papas sixties singing group and spent the year speaking their lyrics in place of normal conversation. As a big fan of the group, I was just a tad jealous that he didn't share that part with me. I could have handled that.

My friend's special little fourth grader thought he was a chicken and had imaginary chickens that surrounded him. He constantly clucked and clucked in class. Occasionally, he squawked and announced he was about to lay an egg. My friend tried many things to try to get him to stop, with varying success. Sometimes requesting that he put his chickens back in their pen would work. But the problem seemed to be getting worse as the year dragged on.

One day, several months into the school year, she had totally had it. Fed up with the constant distraction and at her wit's end, she pulled out an imaginary gun, pretended to shoot his chickens, and informed him that his chickens could no longer cluck because they were all dead. And he had better not bring any more chickens to class because she would shoot them too. At first, he was paralyzed with shock. Then he quietly cried a bit. But after that, his chickens disappeared completely.

ANIMAL CORPSES AND OTHER WEIRD
SHIT KIDS BRING TO SCHOOL

J. MORRIS

A TEACHER FRIEND OF MINE SENT ME A VIDEO OF HER assistant principal bashing a backpack against a wall at school. Apparently, a little girl had put a squirrel corpse in there on the way to school and the AP wanted to make sure it was dead before he opened the bag. This got me thinking about weird shit kids bring to school, so I asked my followers to share some stories. I was not disappointed.

- Several kids have put a live, stray cat in their backpacks on the way to school and kept them in there or hid them in a locker
- A "Barbie necklace" that was actually her dad's cock ring (*I felt gross just typing that*)
- A kindergartener brought her mom's wedding ring and lost it in the sandbox
- Dead animals including snakes, cats, squirrels, birds, fish, rabbits, mice, foxes, frogs and even a baby goat
- Animal skeletons or skulls
- Live cats, rabbits, fish, hamsters, guinea pigs,

hedgehogs, hermit crabs, chickens, turtles, small dogs, snails, lizards, ferrets, tarantulas, cockroaches, a bearded dragon, baby opossums, baby bats, and snakes from home
- Vibrators and dildos
- A used condom that a kindergartener thought was a balloon
- A kindergartener brought in a gun and another brought in a (non-active) grenade
- Mom's sex dice
- A bottle of vodka and a can of White Claw
- Thong underwear
- A girl kept dirty tampons in a Ziploc bag (*barf, I know*)
- Raw chicken wings
- Grandma's ashes
- A second grader put her newborn baby brother in a plastic bag and brought him to school to show her friends. When the teacher called the mom, she had already called the police because she thought the baby was kidnapped.
- On the way to school a student stopped by the scene of a woman who had jumped in front of a train. He took her mandible and brought it to school.
- A breast implant
- A kid brought in a beehive that she thought was empty. The dormant bees woke up later that day and infested the school gym.
- Dentures
- A book of sex positions
- Used Q-Tips
- Newborn brother's poop-filled diaper

- A frozen cougar in a trash bag
- A third grader brought in a sandwich bag full of marijuana
- A pig's tongue in a Cool Whip container
- Fried chicken in a kid's pocket
- Grandma's used insulin syringe
- Escort cards from Vegas
- Mom's rent money, which the student tried to use to buy rare Pokémon cards
- Two cans of clam sauce and a box of raw spaghetti
- An artillery shell
- A kindergartner was carrying a wrench. When asked why, he said, "My mom told me to."
- Crack
- A student brought in a human skull that her dog had dug up. She thought it was a Halloween decoration but it was an actual human skull. The cops swarmed her house that night and it turned out to be the skull of a local missing man. (*It happened in Little River County, Arkansas if you want to Google it.*)
- A giant pump bottle of KY Jelly that the student put on her desk. She thought it was hand sanitizer and offered it around.
- A $700 money order that was his Grandma's bond money
- A kid brought his entire terrarium with his iguana inside. He plugged in the heat lamp and lighting during gym class. Gave no explanation whatsoever.
- Live baby bunnies in a lunchbox
- A stuffed deer... the entire thing

- $5000 in cash. He took it from his mom's dresser and started handing out $100 bills to his classmates. (*Hey kid! Can I have some?*)
- A folding knife in a hidden compartment in a Bible
- Fried chicken wings in a Trapper Keeper
- A third grader tried to give his mom's wedding ring to his girlfriend
- Heroin needles

Weird things kids brought for Show and Tell:

- Dog poop (he thought it was cool how you could see the carrots in it)
- Dad's porn DVD
- A live chicken on a leash
- A real human brain in a Ziploc bag (Dad was a neurologist)
- Mom's dirty undies
- A polaroid of a woman giving a BJ

WHAT DID YOU THINK YOUR SALARY WAS FOR?

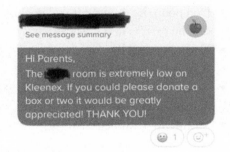

SOMETIMES IT GETS IN

BRIDGET O'NEILL, PHOENIX, ARIZONA

I'VE BEEN A CLASSROOM TEACHER FOR 27 YEARS. I started my teaching career in Parker, Arizona–a little desert town on the banks of the Colorado River. There was one student, among many, who I found particularly wonderful. He was humble, smart, kind– just a good kid overall. My own little boy was a toddler at the time. And I couldn't help but wonder how my little Michael would grow up. One day, I conveyed to this particularly good student of mine that I hoped my son would grow up to be like him someday: well-rounded, capable, kind, and gentle. I didn't think much of it because I usually try to acknowledge gifts and positive traits in my students.

Fast-forward 25 years: Facebook helped that kid find me. He looked me up where I was currently teaching and emailed me, hoping he had found the right person. He proceeded to tell me how much it meant to him that I stated what I did about my own hopes for my son, that he had met with some success and failure, but that, basically, he wanted to tell me what a positive impact I had had on him.

I bawled and went about teaching the next day with a significantly brighter smile in my first hour.

INTERESTING MIX OF TOPICS

Heh I've been noticing ▓▓▓ va jay jay is red and raw . I'm going try a tissue box with toilet paper in it at home and see if this helps with getting her to wipe and if works over weekend I'll send one in . Thanks
Also do they have any special activities for next two months
And I know your birthday coming up
Why size are you in pants and top thank you

ARE YOU A PROFESSIONAL?

ANONYMOUS

I HAD A SELECTIVELY MUTE STUDENT IN FOURTH GRADE who was silent for three years. Her case was never looked into or classified because it "didn't affect her grades," but it drastically affected her life. As a 10-year-old, she peed her pants because she couldn't open her mouth to ask to use the bathroom. I worked with her all year, giving her nonverbal leadership tasks to encourage her self-esteem. I also journaled with her back and forth a few times a week, so I could "talk" to her and get to know her. I told her I wanted to help her get over her fear of speaking before she moved onto middle school.

She wrote to me that she would speak on March 1st and she would say one word to the class. At this point, all of the teachers and students in the school knew she was mute because she had been for so long. Everyone was so excited for her to speak. March 1st came around, and she was too scared to talk. I continued to encourage and support her. Eventually, in May, she finally opened her mouth and said hello to our class and me. I ended up making a calendar and tracking with her how many times she spoke each day and

made it into a game. It got to the point where she was partic-
ipating in class and communicating on a totally normal
level.

Graduation came around in June, and I needed to select
one student to make an announcement during the cere-
mony. I chose her, and she nervously accepted. We prac-
ticed for weeks, holding an index card and enunciating into
a microphone. She stood in front of almost 400 people and
made an announcement, and she got a standing ovation.
Her mother came to me and cried and touched my feet (as a
sign of respect in her culture), saying I'm the best thing that
ever happened to her. She went on to middle school,
competed in spelling bees, is on the soccer team, and is a
member of student council. She still writes to me now, three
years later, telling me that I helped her believe in herself
and gave her the confidence to speak out loud. It was the
proudest moment of my teaching career.

My colleague's son was in my class, and she didn't like
the way I taught. Her child was failing because she told
him he didn't have to do homework or study for tests. She
didn't agree with the curriculum I was using (which was
given to me by the district), so she would give him different
work to complete. Inevitably he failed everything because
he wasn't learning what I was teaching. She was best
friends with the principal, and although my principal gave
me high marks on my observations, she said I needed to be
put on a Corrective Action Plan because parents had
complaints. When I asked her to share some of those
complaints with me, she only cited the one student who
was failing. When I brought up the fantastic progress I had
helped the other (formerly mute) student make, she said
nothing.

The next day, in the middle of teaching, my principal

called my classroom phone and said, "Hello. Are you a professional?" I answered, "Yes. Is there an issue?"

"A note was found in the teacher's lounge about head-phones. This note went home with students and parents, as well as the PTA. They are calling saying that teachers should not be sending home handwritten letters. I know it was you, so I just want to know why you would do some-thing like this?"

"Oh, I never send home handwritten letters," I replied. "I sent home my headphones letter a few months ago, and it was typed up. That wasn't mine."

"I have proof that it's yours," she spat back at me. "The parents said it was yours. They called the board office and complained, and now my head is being chopped off for your unprofessional behavior!"

"Again, I don't know why my name was mentioned because I did *not* send that letter home."

"Let me see how I can get you and our entire school out of this mess," she said. And then added, "If you are not asked back next year, *this is why*." Then she slammed the phone down.

I was mortified. I started questioning myself like, *shit, did I write that letter?* I went back to my files and saw a copy of my typed-out letter and thought *damn, am I crazy?* I went to her office three times that day to get to the bottom of it, but the secretaries turned me away every time. Finally, towards the end of the day, she aggressively called me to her office over the school-wide intercom. I went into her office and she did not even look up from her paperwork to address me. "Why have you been looking for me all day?" she said with a nasty attitude.

"Umm, I'm trying to clarify the situation you called me about earlier. I never wrote that letter. I have the letter that I sent home earlier in the year to show you." She shooed me away with her hand and said, "Yeah, yeah, yeah, I found out who it was. You're dismissed."

I spoke to my coworkers about it, and they were all confused as to why she accused me in the first place. They all knew who wrote that letter from early that morning.

I was fired soon after, one day before receiving tenure. When I asked for a reason why, the principal sighed and said, "You're just not enough of a professional."

103

THE INTERLOPERS

@RATEYOURPD

"WHAT LETTER SYMBOLIZES YOUR JOURNEY AND WHY?" I ask. We sit in the middle of the classroom, in a circle, with just our chairs. One student says, "R for rude," there's also an O for over-thinker; another is I for inferior. Several students in the class chose "F" for failure.

My students' lips tremble. Their voices crack. Their eyes begin to tear. Some take the time to explain their letter, others just reveal it and sit down. For the first time in a long time, I am getting to know them, understand them, and see them. Their impulse is to share themselves with me, unreserved and without hesitation.

Literature is a force.

Then, in the middle of our magical fucking moment, I hear the jingling of keys and *they* walk in. *"They"* are my principal and the Assistant Superintendent of Secondary Schools and *they* like to *watch... a lot.*

The principal walks to the back of the room and sits down next to one of my students. He whispers into her ear, making her visibly uncomfortable. The other guy is the

Fucking-Principal-of-all-Fucking-Principals. He takes a picture of my whiteboard.

"Fuck," I think to myself. "I didn't update my learning objective and agenda from this morning."

I found out about the district Fuck Face's visit 10 minutes before it happened. It wasn't even 11 AM and already a student told me his same-age cousin shot and killed himself the night before. I ran out of my class to find someone to help the student. I ran back across campus to teach my classroom of 36 students about symbolism in literature. I conducted the first two periods in perfect synchronicity with my whiteboard's written objective and agenda, while students also collaborated in academic discourse using *Depth of Knowledge* levels 2-3.

Fuck Face camouflages something sinister beneath his eyes. He is thinking. Little Fuck Face, my principal, inquires harder into the student's ear.

The observable student engagement and authentic academic discourse doesn't match with the objective and agenda written on my whiteboard. They like to judge a lot. I am pissed.

And they just ruined my *Authentic Transformative Teaching Experience.* District Fuck Faces are the administrators, the invaders, the interlopers, Fuck-Ah-Fuck-Ahs, creeping into our rooms uninvited. But Fuck Faces missed the first part of the lesson, when I modeled my Scarlet Letter "R" for Resist.

I get up from the circle and walk to the whiteboard. I point to District Fuck Face to join me. We have history. Last year District Fuck Face and I exchanged words because I asked too many irrelevant questions at a Professional Development like, "Have *you* ever taught in a Title 1 high school before?"

I say, "Good morning, Doctor Fuck-Ah-Fuck-Ah. I know the academic discourse doesn't match my board. I am improvising. Half of my class is unexpectedly missing today. Taking a health survey. We weren't notified," I look at my Fuck Face Principal.

He smiles and in a sing-song voice replies, "Collecting data on student health is important." I shake my head, "These kids have a right to an education that is of value to them. Tools they can examine their own lives with and stuff, you know? I am working hard trying to do it. Help me. Support me. Stop the constant interruptions."

"Oh, *no*! No judgments here! We're here just to observe," my principal says. They turn to leave. The administrators pause at the door and turn around.

"Dr. Fuck-Ah-Fuck-Ah, by the way, great suit! I can tell it's like custom. *Tailor made*. Fits you nice. And I'm a Union Rep. now! See ya!" I wave.

Fucking-Fuck-Ah-Fuck-Ahs.

104

TAKE MY WORD FOR IT, PLEASE

ANONYMOUS

I WAS SITTING IN THE TEACHERS' LOUNGE ONE DAY when I got an airdropped file from a student sent to my computer. This had never happened to me before and stupidly, I opened it. It was porn, and it started auto-playing on my computer for everyone else in the lounge to hear. It wasn't your average porn either. It involved explosive diarrhea. I couldn't eat again for over 24 hours.

I explained the situation to an administrator on the phone and he said, "Can you send it to me?" I told him that he *definitely* did not want to see what I had seen. He continued to insist that I send him the porn. "We need to see it to verify that it is pornography." I couldn't help but laugh. "Trust me. *You don't want to see this.* Take my word for it." Next, the admin asked me to meet him after school. I entered his office, and the other assistant principal was there along with the principal. I was forced to log into my account, find the file, and play the explosive diarrhea porn for them. No one said anything except the principal who said, "Yep. That's definitely porn."

They looked at the security footage to see who was close enough to the teachers' lounge to have sent it. It was easy to figure out, and the student only received half a day of in-school suspension. That was the entire consequence for sending his teacher explosive diarrhea porn.

CORRECT YOUR TONE

To: English Teacher
From: Whett Faartz
Subject: Yo

Hey Ms. do you wanna send me the worksheets
we're doing in class this week or nah

To: Whett Faartz
From: English teacher
Subject: Re: Yo

Hi Whett,
When you are emailing your teachers you
should use a more formal tone/vocabulary and
correct spelling and grammar mistakes as well.

To: English Teacher
From: Whett Faartz
Subject: Re: Re: Yo

Thou finest professorial purveyor of English knowledge, I sincerely apologize for my previous vocabulary. So can I have those worksheets or nah?

FUN IS A CRIME

SAM, ARIZONA

My campus sometimes feels like a cesspool—a cesspool swirling with unreasonable site and district admin, and state requests. But I suppose we're all wading through that waist-deep swamp full of bullshit demands.

The request this time? Multiple emails in my inbox read: NO PARTIES. NO FOOD. NO MUSIC. NO MOVIES. NO STREAMING. STAY ACADEMIC DURING FINALS WEEK.

So, despite that unreasonable request (because what am I supposed to do with kids for two days when they have finished all their district assessments, and the district refuses to give teachers access to their mandated final test that could potentially help prepare them for it but whatever), a moment of joy sparked in my classroom. A girl took all of her classmates' sticky-note annotations and turned them into a piñata. The weird kid brought a rope. I already had a stick from a former student's project and a leftover candy stash from a recent contest. That was some *carpe-diem-shit* right there.

We'd just finished reading *Lord of the Flies*, with most

agreeing that humanity was doomed. But here they were, pushing desks aside and ordering the tall kids to stand on the desks and hold the rope from opposite sides of the room. They were lining up, smallest to biggest, teaching each other the song. One even knew to close the blinds. Finally, a little fun. And it was the best kind of fun—spontaneous and innocent. But the subject lines of those emails ran through my mind. I began rattling off rules to them, killing the mood —or vibe-checking them.

But despite my protests, the party was in full swing. Tiny 15-year-old girls began beating the shit out of the piñata. I had never seen so much joy in my classroom. Suddenly the phone rang, and the class collectively let out a shush as I answered. A neighboring teacher asked if there was a fight. I said, "No, just a piñata." He said, "Right on." The party was back in full swing.

When the candy hit the floor, a handful of teenagers jumped to gather it. They were laughing happily. But all I could see were those subject lines and the mess all over the floor. We could all see the mess. I looked around the room, and kids started looking away. Who was going to clean this up?

"For every handful of confetti, you get five extra credit points!" I declared. And then all 31 kids swarmed the floor and began thrusting their handfuls of garbage in my face until I confirmed that they had gotten their points. The bell rang, and they left gleefully, knowing to keep our class party on the down-low.

But I suppose that's what bothered me the most. During the piñata beating, I was keeled over from laughter with tears in my eyes. Teenagers were jumping up and down like they were little children again. Beforehand (and afterward, if I'm honest), I felt like a criminal—that I needed to hide this collective bonding experience and probably one of the happiest moments in my teaching career like I was a beaten dog or something. That's the real "teacher misery": when we're so belittled and micromanaged that we begin to feel like fun in the classroom is a crime.

107

HONEST REPORT CARD COMMENTS

J. MORRIS

WHEN WE ARE ASKED TO WRITE REPORT CARD comments, we know we have to sugarcoat them as much as possible. There must be a nice, productive way of saying even the most negative thing. The student sits around all day, staring out the window, eating boogers? "Has quite an appetite for life!" The student cannot stop yelling out inappropriate comments about the teacher's body parts? "Excellent at self-expression!" You can't come out and say the truth. It's just not allowed.

So I asked my teacher followers to share the comments they'd really like to write on some student report cards and here are the best ones:

- When he's sitting on your couch at 40, please remember I tried!
- Needs to practice saying, "Would you like fries with that?" as career prep.
- I encourage him to take a short break from video games to shower, which will lead to overall better hygiene and improved social skills.

- Needs a mental evaluation ASAP.
- We find maggots in and around her desk every day.
- She can miss up to nine days this semester without losing credit, just FYI.
- Good luck with this one!
- I have to hold his hand in the hallway because he cannot stop touching others.
- Probably going to be a porn star.
- Hopefully the family has some inheritance lined up for him.
- A good kick in the ass would go a long way.
- She says she will be either a pediatric surgeon or an Instagram influencer–whichever happens first. I don't have much hope for either.
- I want him in class as little as he wants to be there.
- I don't even know what your kid looks like because he has never shown up.
- Medication please.
- Is in an ongoing romantic relationship with the classroom fan.
- Obviously needs more attention at home.
- Has a potential future in the custodial arts.
- Your child is like a blender without the lid.
- Continues to call me "bro" and stares blankly when given simple directions such as "sit down."
- Would be a great seat filler at a funeral.
- Class participation consists mainly of farts.
- Says, "This school is a fucking prison" so often that I would like to visit him when he ends up in one and ask, "So was it?"

- Couldn't count his balls and get the same number twice.
- Smells like rotten camel shit.
- A pleasure to have absent.
- Potential serial killer.
- Has the I.Q. of a chair.
- Doesn't do shit, but at least he isn't an asshole.
- Annoyingly perfect attendance.
- Picks his scabs and eats them.
- He finally learned to read. Hopefully, that will help him in prison.
- Too much body spray, not enough bathing.
- Wastes so much oxygen he should apologize to trees.
- Birth control highly advised for your family.
- Your child is the reason alcohol should be a tax deduction for teachers.
- Has the potential to be the next Unibomber.
- A very friendly girl, always shares her milkshake with the boys during recess.
- My heart fills with joy when your child is absent.
- Great by Friday, but comes back to school a terror on Monday. It's your fault, Patricia!
- Has a lot to say but has no sense of timing, appropriateness, or any other social skill required for real-world success.
- Humps the radiator but pretends he is sharpening his pencil.
- Someone's gotta dig ditches.
- The barking in class has become less frequent, but the howling is problematic.

- If being an asshole was a skill, your child does it at a mastery level.
- I hope he's not afraid of the dark because there are definitely no lights on upstairs.
- I think he'd really benefit from homeschooling.
- Enjoy fighting all her battles for her and defending all of her poor choices because you're going to be doing it for the foreseeable future.
- Least disruptive when sleeping.
- Complete opposite of pleasure to have in class.
- Going to be a fantastic trophy wife/husband someday.
- He watches porn on his phone in class. Please buy him headphones!

108

TMI

ANONYMOUS

THERE ARE THREE WEEKS LEFT OF THE SEMESTER. ONE student has only shown up for class six times the entire semester, but I'm willing to let him make up enough work to pass. I call home to let his parents know what is going on, and mom answers.

"Hi, Mrs. Dover. This is Ben's math teacher. I'm calling to let you know that Ben is failing. But-"

"Yeah, my son thinks he's a man, but he is really just a lazy-ass piece of shit. He just sits at home all day playing video games."

"Yes, well, even though he hasn't been here much this semester-"

"He doesn't understand what life is really like because his girlfriend pays for everything."

"Yes, that is definitely a problem. But it isn't too late for Ben to-"

"One time, he wanted to borrow my truck, and I said no, and he spit right in my face. A big wet one!"

"That is terrible."

"But I spit back in his face and slapped the shit outta him!"

"Oh my."

"I told him he wasn't a real man!"

"Right."

"For a while I was dropping him off at school to make sure he got there, but he would just walk home after I drove away."

"Is that right? Well, we really need to make sure he attends class for the next three weeks and does all of the makeup work because if not-"

"I wasn't feeling well one day and left work early. I went into my room to take a nap, and he was having sex with his girlfriend in my bed!"

"*Woah!*"

"The nerve of him! Is that what real men do!? Have sex in their mother's bed!?"

"Mrs. Dover, I just wanted to let you know that there is still time for Ben to pass my class. But I have other phone calls to make, so..."

"I made him buy me new sheets."

"Thank you for your time. Goodbye."

A LOVE LETTER OF SORTS

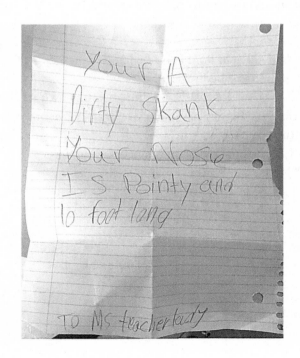

DUE PROCESS

T.S., BOSTON, MASSACHUSETTS

IT WAS THE TUESDAY BEFORE CHRISTMAS BREAK. IT snowed in the morning, and then there was freezing rain. In our K-8 school, the middle schoolers decided to open a piercing parlor in the girls' bathroom. It was about an hour before dismissal. The girls were sprawled out on the disgusting bathroom floor, and the ring leader was piercing belly buttons. They knew enough to know that they needed to sterilize the needle, so someone brought a lighter. They even knew that they needed to sterilize the skin, so they swiped a bottle of hand sanitizer from a nearby classroom. Apparently, the only thing they didn't know is that hand sanitizer is flammable.

As they performed the piercings, a small fire started. They tried to put the fire out but couldn't. An adult smelled the smoke and ran into the bathroom. She started stomping on the fire, and then her boot caught on fire. An administrator walked by, heard screaming, saw smoke, and pulled the fire alarm. Someone got on the intercom and said, "This is not a drill! Evacuate the building!" I quickly got my eighth graders out of the building. The poor kindergarteners had just been ripped from their naps. The whole school waited outside in the freezing rain with no coats for hours.

The fire department finally got everything under control and gave the all-clear to let us back in.

As the kids started to settle down, there was a commotion outside the classroom, and it was one of five fights that day. This one involved the girls who began the piercing salon and fire because one accused another of snitching to admin. The fight spilled out of the school and into the street, and the girls almost got hit by a car! One girl began physically assaulting the police officer who was in the building after responding to the fire. She was eventually cuffed and put into an ambulance.

The next day, every kid who was in a fight and every kid involved with the fire was back in school (yes, even the girl who was taken away in cuffs). When we asked the principal why these students were allowed back at school after putting us all in danger, he replied, "Well, they have to get their 'due process,' and we can't do anything until a hearing happens with their families, and they couldn't do it today. They are still entitled to their education."

The hearings happened on Thursday morning, and the girls got suspended for two days. So basically they just got an extra-long vacation. And me? I got the flu from standing in the freezing rain for two hours with no coat, and it lasted my entire holiday vacation.

SHIT ADMINISTRATORS SAY

J. MORRIS

ADMINISTRATORS WERE TEACHERS ONCE, BUT probably long ago, and not for very long. They frequently forget where they came from and what it was like to be a teacher. Admins love to complain about how hard their job is while being paid 3-4 times more as a young teacher, who is *undoubtedly* working much harder than most of them. They are usually *way* too involved or too hands-off, and I personally prefer the later. Many admins are merely looking to move up the chain of command in their district, so they are afraid to discipline kids, afraid of backlash from parents, and afraid of most kinds of confrontation. They generally reward the people they are afraid of, punish those who they can trust to get the job done by piling on more work, and enjoy feeling a false sense of power from pushing around other adults who they perceive as below them. These types of admins are just plain pathetic, in my opinion.

Are they *all* like this? No. Some actually care about the students and teachers, and took the job to make the school a better place. But many people who are drawn to those kinds of positions have power dynamic issues and gain their entire sense of self-worth from this perceived sense of importance. Just look at these real quotes from admins around the country, trying to be all-knowing and super important:

"I know we all spend money out of our pockets for our classrooms and students but we need to make sure we are all making our yearly tax donations to our school as well so that we can have funding to do things."

"Exhaustion is proof that you care!"

"Dear teachers, there will be places in today's assembly where I will need a standing ovation to occur. I am hoping that it will happen anyway, but I will hand out scripts to teachers to make sure that it happens when I need it to."

"Each and every one of you is replaceable."

"The fact that a student was using their phone in your class tells me that you do not care about your students or their education."

"We need to have a grade level meeting today about the grade level meeting we are having tomorrow."

"You don't need to worry about retirement. You are young and you can get a sugar daddy."

"During your (twenty minute) lunch, I need you to personally escort this student to lunch and then pick him up and escort him to his next class, *every day*."

"Student tardiness is not my issue. It is *your* issue."

"I read your office referral and I met with the student. He says he didn't do it so it's kind of your word against his at this point."

"If they need notebooks, you can buy them for your students for only fifty cents at Walmart. Don't ask us, because we don't have any to give."

"It's not my job to care how you feel."

"He didn't really eat a dead bird. He chewed it a bit and spit it out."

"The latest thinking in education is that there is no need for committees so let's just think of a new name for ours."

"I know you are looking for guidance as far as the behavior problems in your classes. My best advice is to go home and drink some wine."

(*Teacher tells admin that a student airdropped a picture of a vagina to her phone.*) "Why are you letting them use their cell phones in class?"

"I have your back until the parents call to complain."

"The student didn't bite you. His tooth scraped against your arm."

"In this school, there are no longer consequences."

"I know the heat is broken and it is very cold in the school but staff needs to set an example for the students by *not* wearing coats, jackets, fleece, or any type of outerwear."

"If students keep misbehaving after all of the interventions that is when it is the most important to greet them at your door by name!"

"In this school we don't ever tell parents 'no.'"

"I know you are upset that we took your planning period for hallway duty but that's what weekends are for!"

Superintendent: "Teachers are servants."

"The needs are with the parents who threaten lawsuits, not with the actual students."

"Let's celebrate breast awareness month!"

"There is no reason to ever request leave for a doctor's appointment. That is what summers are for."

"If a student runs out of the classroom you absolutely must run after them. I don't care if you are nine months pregnant. Do you have a doctor's note saying you can't run? Then you should be able to."

"All of the tape you have put on the chairs is gumming them up. We can't use goo-gone because it can be toxic to some kids. Can you send a few students down at the end of the day to help scrape the goo with a razor blade?"

"You are no longer allowed to sit during parent conferences. It's not professional. The parents can sit, but you stand."

"Your wife is expecting again? You should have called Mr. Snip-it like I did after my second child."

(*Student refuses to take notes in class*) "Well we're not training him to be a secretary."

"If there is an active shooter in the building just tell your kids to keep working."

"Be mindful of dress code. No one wants to see your muffin top."

"Sorry we overbooked the gym. Can you give your test in the janitor's closet?"

"It is inappropriate for a girl's bra strap to be showing. So if you notice it, just tuck it in for her."

"You need to eat, sleep and breathe this job. You need to run yourself into the ground. If not, you aren't doing it correctly."

"A parent complained that not all of the teachers looked happy during the holiday show. Smiling during the show is mandatory."

"I felt relieved when I saw you crying after that parent conference. I was worried that you didn't have feelings at all."

(*From superintendent*) "I reached out to parents and asked them to consider a donation to our ed. foundation in lieu of holiday gifts for teachers. The response has been excellent so far! If you receive an email letting you know that a donation has been made in your name, it is very important that you send the family a handwritten thank you note."

EXPERT PUDDING EATER

JENNIFER, ILLINOIS

IT WAS MY FIRST YEAR TEACHING NINTH GRADE English. To preview our next unit, I handed out a survey with different topics. Students had to indicate if they were an expert, had some knowledge, or had minimal experience about something. At the bottom, there was a free response question that asked the students to indicate anything else they felt they were an expert at.

One of my students had the accommodation of having a scribe. I went through the survey with him and wrote down his answers. When we got to the free response, he said, "Yeah, write that I am an expert at eating P-U-S-S-Y." He actually spelled out the *pussy* part, so there was no confusion. I tried to remain calm and simply told him that his response was not appropriate. A look of amusement came over his face, and he said, "That's what I want you to write, cuz it's true." Then he gave me a creepy little smile. "I am *not* going to write that, so I guess we will leave it blank," I responded. "Will I lose points for not answering the question?" he asked. "Yes," I said, and got up and moved as far away from the student as possible.

Naturally, I contacted home to report what happened, but apparently, the student anticipated that I would call his mom, and he had called her during lunch. Before I could complete a sentence, she started screaming at me that she already knew what had happened in class. She said I was wrong for not writing his answer, and that he *obviously* did not know how to spell *pudding*. I had to meet with the mom, the kid, and the principal and defend myself. I insisted that he knew what he was spelling and meant to be inappropriate, but the mom said I was discriminating against her son for not being able to spell. The principal agreed with her and lectured me about what is appropriate to call parents about.

Meanwhile, for the rest of the year, the kid slyly licked his lips and winked at me during each and every class.

A GLIMMER

BECKY PEABODY, RHODE ISLAND

I HAD A ROUGH CHILDHOOD AND A NEGLECTFUL mother (she chose drugs before her kids, often). I'm at the point in my life where I'm beyond it. I think it's made me an excellent teacher and a strong, independent woman. However, I get weird on Mother's Day. Too many people gave me crap over the years for not acknowledging my own mother on this holiday because apparently it is required.

I taught in an inner-city school for a while, and over the years, I bonded with a core group of kids, many of whom had their own sad mom or dad story. One year on the day after Mother's Day, while I was being a grump and trying to eat lunch in silent solitude and misery, these four kids who I'd had for three and four years at that point, and who called me "Mom," burst in on my sad little lunch with chocolates, flowers and a card that read, "Our family tree may look different, but it's the most loving and accepting place I know." They wrote the sweetest notes inside about how my being like a mother to them at school had changed their worlds. I sobbed. These are kids I nagged about low grades, scolded for poor decision-making, and put my hands on my hips and made "I'm disappointed in you" faces at. These are kids who I still keep in touch with about college and work, who still reach out to me to see how I'm doing. On the hard days, I look at my card, proudly on display on my bulletin board, and I remember why we do this: *For the kids. Always for the kids.*

114

2000, 2010, 2020

IT'S INTERESTING HOW QUICKLY THE TEACHING profession has changed over the last 20 years. While I am grateful to the internet for giving me a platform and a voice, I also think it has ruined a lot of kids' attention spans and sense of reality and has definitely made my profession 50 million times harder. I asked my followers to describe how teaching and kids have changed from the year 2000 (around the time I graduated high school) to 2010 (a few years after I started teaching) to today (2020).

2000- Stop passing notes.
2010- Stop texting.
2020- Are you seriously watching Netflix right now?

2000- Fight after school.
2010- Cyberbullying.
2020- Post fight videos online to see who gets the most likes.

2000- Not teacher's fault if student fails.

2010- What are you doing to make sure your students don't fail?
2020- Your student is failing so you are ineffective and need more training!

2000- Reads the novel.
2010- Pretends to have read the novel.
2020- "No I didn't read it! That shit looks boring!"

2000- "Sorry I misbehaved."
2010- "Suck my dick, I don't care."
2020- Student hits teacher, parents defend kid.

2000- Student receives two day suspension from school for using cell phone at lunch to call mom.
2010- You have to ask students to put phones away several times, but they do it without much of a fight.
2020- Student who is failing every class has brand new iPhone 11 after multiple referrals for looking at porn on phone in class.

2000- "I can't fail this class. I need to get into college."
2010- "Whatever, fail me. College degrees ain't worth shit anyway."
2020- "You can't fail me. Fix my grade or I'll complain to admin."

2000- Students order pizza from payphone.
2010- Students call Domino's from phone in bathroom.
2020- Students order pizza using UberEats app right in the middle of class.

2000- Student prints out inappropriate pic in black and white and leaves it on my desk.
2010- Student emails me inappropriate pics from anonymous email account.
2020- Student airdrops me porn.

2000- "We're watching a movie? Yay!"
2010- "Well, what movie is it? Is it going to be boring?"
2020- Teacher plays movie and students put earbuds in and watch things on their phones.

2000- Smokes weed in school and gets expelled.
2010- Smokes weed in school and gets suspended.
2020- Smokes weed in school again and might get detention.

2000- "Can we work in groups?"
2010- "Can we work with a friend?"
2020- "Can I work with my earbuds in?"

2000- Rolls eyes at teacher.
2010- Curses at teacher.
2020- Throws furniture at teacher.

2000- Kid has lice and gets sent home.
2010- Kid has lice and is not sent home but other parents are informed.
2020- It is the kid's right to have lice and you should not judge or embarrass them.

115

JUST A LITTLE LEAK

ANONYMOUS

I WORK IN A CLASSROOM FOR STUDENTS WITH SPECIAL needs. Our classroom is in a trailer outside of the school building due to overcrowding. We were only in the trailer for a month before students had blown fuses, put multiple holes through the drywall, and flooded the entire trailer.

A student hit a water pipe in the tiny bathroom in the trailer, causing it to bust. My teaching assistant ran into the bathroom and yelled for help as she quickly attempted to scoop gushing water into a tiny bucket and dump it into the toilet. I heard her scream and opened the door, and she was up to her ankles in water already. I got a bigger bucket to catch water, and we kept scooping the water and dumping it, trying not to let the flood spread, while the students laughed and cheered. We called the office for help. They didn't seem to understand how serious the situation was, and no one came. They thought we had a minor leak.

After frantically trying to stop the leak, we gave up and watched the water spread quickly across the entire classroom floor as the kids jumped and splashed. They were having the time of their lives. My teaching assistant ran into the building and found a custodian to come and help. He walked in and yelled, "Oh hell no! Did you turn off the water!?" As calmly as I could, I showed him the busted pipe and said I didn't know where the water valve was to shut it off. He looked at the water gushing into the bathroom and said, "I ain't paid to be a plumber!" and he disappeared.

A second custodian came a few minutes later and was brave enough to go under the trailer (there are several families of wild animals living underneath) to search for the main water shut-off valve. No one knew where it was or if the trailers even had one, and he found no solution.

We continued to scoop water with trash cans and were soaked from head to toe. Finally, a third custodian came and knew that the valve was in the tiny closet next to the bathroom. Eventually, the water stopped. Soon after, the principal walked in and said, "Well they sure underestimated the little leak in your trailer, huh? It looks like you tried to make a swimming pool!" Then he laughed and walked out.

For the next month, we were without a classroom. Every morning I was told to "find a space that's available" to put my class into. We rarely found an empty space and ended up in the cafeteria. The following year they tried to put me back into a trailer, and I told the principal that if I had to have my class in a trailer again, I needed life preservers. All he said was, "I don't get it."

116

BITCHBYE

Ok...SO YOU TELLING ME MY SON NOT
SMART ENOUGH TO FORMULATE
ANSWERS AS HE DID ON THE TEST?
#BITCHBYE

YOU CAN FEEL FREE TO HAVE AN
ADMINISTRATOR CALL ME OR DO
WHATEVER YOU SEE FIT. IT'S TOO EARLY
IN MY WORKDAY TO ENTERTAIN SUCH
FOOLISHNESS!!! I RESENT YOU
ASSUMPTION THAT MY SON ISN'T CAPABLE
OF SUCH WORK. THAT'S EXACTLY HOW DA
FUCK YOUR EMAIL READS!!! IT
WARRANTED THIS TYPE OF RESPONSE.
FYI- MY 1ST AMENDMENT CONSTITUTIONAL
RIGHTS ALLOW ME FREEDOM OF SPEECH
IN THE RARE INSTANCE YOU TAKE ISSUE
WITH THIS RESPONSE!! HOW DO I KNOW
YOU DIDN'T GOOGLE THIS DUMB ASS
EMAIL? EXACTLY.

117

LET IT GO

CATHY RILEY, NEW HAMPSHIRE

In 2013, I worked for a very insular high school in a small town in Southeastern Virginia. This town had one high school, and it was so small that I taught the entire 11th grade. This was around the time that students were discovering the joy that is Snapchat. They would always tell me I needed a Snapchat, and I spent a lot of time telling them that taking pictures in my room with their phones was a recipe for a referral because I did not want to hear about my classroom being on the Interweb.

Sometime in the spring, one of my students came to me clearly upset. She told me that she had something to show me, but she didn't want to. I assured her that I was a safe person to share things with, so she finally pulled out her phone. She had saved a screenshot of a Snapchat that had circulated among students at the school. The picture was of me teaching, unaware I was being photographed. I tend to talk with my hands, which gave the student who took the film all the setup he needed. The photographer photoshopped me holding a giant black dildo and then sent it around. It was pretty realistic looking, and it quickly went "viral" at our school.

The girl who showed me the picture also told me who had created the image, though she made me swear I wouldn't give her up as the snitch. I went to my principal, explained the situation, showed her the picture, and said that I knew who had done it. She did not react in any way to the image (which was quite shocking.) She simply looked at me calmly and replied, "Since we have no way to *prove* where the image started, I can't address it. You'll just have to let it go." In my mind, there were so many ways that she could have taken care of this. She could have called kids in for questioning. She should have checked the phone of the kid in question. But any attempt I made to get her to take more of an interest in my situation seemed to irritate her.

I did let it go. After that incident, which was only one of about four incidents where the ACLU or the HRC or other third party needed to get involved, my wife and I decided to move to New Hampshire. It's been six years, and the dildo pic hasn't resurfaced. But I worry about it on a near-weekly basis.

KNOW YOUR NO'S AND ROLLS!

DEAR STAFF,

I feel I need to take a moment to address some dress code concerns now that the weather is getting warmer.

1. Women should not wear clothing that is too tight.

2. Remember the golden rule: if you would wear your outfit at a club or to snag that true love, you probably should NOT wear it at our little school that we all love so much.

3. There is no such thing as "fitums" meaning "one size fits all." We must know our sizes and order correctly because we want to be able to breathe. Emphasizing areas that do not need to be emphasized is not helping us wear the clothes, but instead it's letting others know our NO's and rolls!

PRIVATE DOES NOT MEAN ANONYMOUS

120

PRIVILEGE TO PEE

ANONYMOUS

DURING MY FIRST YEAR OF TEACHING, I TAUGHT IN THE Philadelphia school district. I was a music teacher for grades 9-12. I had a schedule where I had no breaks until 2:30 every day, with a half-hour lunch. Any time I would get my period, have coffee shits, or just generally had the human need to urinate, I would have to wait from 7:30 to 11:33, until my lunch break.

I was continually told that I was required to be at my classroom door (which did not lock) between classes. So running to the bathroom then wasn't an option either. According to every handbook I could find, this was not true, but it was reiterated to me multiple times by admin.

Unfortunately, my classroom door was visible from the principal's office. This made my life absolute hell when students were acting up in the hallway because I would be blamed. It also made the possibility of sneaking to the bathroom impossible.

One day I got my period a week early. It hit hard and fast with some seriously heavy bleeding, the kind that soaks through a tampon in 1-2 hours. I slipped out of my classroom between classes, around 9:30. I had no choice but to bleed through my pants or slip away and take less than three minutes to clean myself up.

I called the office three times before the previous class had ended. I asked for someone to stand in my room so I could use the bathroom. Nobody picked up. I didn't have a list of other teachers' extensions. I asked students to find an adult, and they couldn't find anybody. My next class only had 15 kids, and I trusted them to be in the classroom alone for three minutes.

While in the bathroom, the bell for the next class rang. I could hear the principal's ear-splitting voice in the hall right by the teacher's bathroom. I had two options: stay and wait for her to go away and risk her seeing my unattended classroom of students or slip out and hope to make it to the classroom while she was occupied.

I decided to try to slip past her immediately. She was talking to a few students when she called out to me, "Excuse me, who is watching your classroom?" I stopped and turned around. "Nobody," I responded. "You know you cannot legally allow students to be in the room alone."

"Yes," I said as politely as possible. "However, I was in the bathroom between periods." The students she was talking to stood there looking amused. "Policy dictates that you must be at your classroom door between classes," she said with a bit of an attitude. "Yes, I know," I said. "However, I called the office and sent students to find somebody to cover my class while I used the bathroom, and nobody came."

"You need to wait then."

Visibly agitated and tired of being undermined in front of students I said, "It's difficult to wait when I need to clean up a lot of blood in my underwear!" The students looked shocked. "Go back to class. And as soon as someone comes to cover your class, see me in my office."

Someone came to cover my class. And I went to see the principal. She told me it was inappropriate to talk about my period in front of students. I asked if my normal, uterus-having bodily functions were inappropriate. She said no. I said that it was inappropriate to even bring me to the point of describing my bodily functions in order to defend myself in front of students.

I told her that she had been bullying me, undermining me in front of students, and denying me normal hygiene and cleanliness standards. She berated me to tears, as my class did absolutely nothing for an entire class period. Later that day, she passive-aggressively emailed a list of all the teachers' classroom extensions to everybody in case of an emergency.

This was the first time I'd ever defended myself to an authority figure in my life. And I'm happy to say that it worked. She pretty much left me alone after that. I left that school after one year and taught at a charter school where I was fired mid-year for failing to sign out during lunch. A year and a half in and I'm done with this profession.

121

OKAY BITCH!

0. Without finding the sums, does the pair of addends have a sum greater than 100? Choose Yes or No.

77 + 12	○ Yes	◉ No
49 + 72	◉ Yes	○ No
16 + 95	◉ Yes	○ No
47 + 46	○ Yes	◉ No

Explain how you decided which pairs have a sum greater than 100.

BC Bitch I used blocks.

IF ONLY THIS CAR WOULD HIT ME

ETHAN WAINWRIGHT, LONDON, ENGLAND

I moved to London from Australia to teach high school and was introduced to the behavior management strategy of daily report cards for students who frequently misbehaved. A traffic light system was used for these reports: green meant you reported to the homeroom teacher at the end of the day, yellow meant you reported to the assistant principal, and red meant you reported to the principal.

A particularly difficult 10th grade girl had to go each day to the assistant principal for a new report card where classroom teachers would rate her behavior for each lesson of the day as either unsatisfactory (red), satisfactory (yellow), or outstanding (green). I didn't know that she had an agreement with the assistant principal that if she received outstanding for her behavior in every lesson for three days in a row, then she would be taken off report.

During my lesson, her behavior wasn't shocking (she managed not to swear at me or throw anything during class), but she did absolutely no work. At the end of the class, she forgot to ask me to sign her report, so she came back during the next period. In the middle of introducing and explaining the science experiment we would be doing, she barged in, interrupted me, and said, "You forgot to sign my report card!"

I had to stop the lesson, knowing that if I asked her to come back, she might start an argument with me. I ticked the box that said "satisfactory," which was generous, considering she did no work and was now interrupting me. She was not happy. At that point, she grabbed the pen that was on a lanyard around my neck and pulled it, snapping the lanyard off. She proceeded to scribble out my tick and place a new one in the "outstanding" box. I went to grab the report card at the same time she did, and we played tug-o-war with the paper until I let go. At this point, she held her report card up in my face and ripped it in two. She then threw both pieces of paper in my face, called me a "cunt" and left the room, slamming the door and taking my pen and broken lanyard with her.

Admin's reply was that her dad was a well-known drug dealer in the area, so she had no boundaries at home, and I just needed to accept her how she was. I remember crossing the road walking from the tube to school the next day, and as I got to the middle of the road, I thought to myself, "I should just stand here and get hit by a car, so I have a good enough reason not to walk through the school gates." That's when I realized I needed to quit!

THESE UPDATES ARE DISGUSTING

A TEACHER SENT AN EMAIL TO HER STUDENTS' PARENTS explaining that she would be sending weekly emails with updates on what the students will be learning and upcoming homework assignments. Here was one parent's response:

"Weekly Parent emails? NO. This is MIDDLE SCHOOL not elementary school. I am disappointed that the youth are not given more respect. I am saddened that you deny them the opportunity to practice responsibility. It is very concerning that you are certain you cannot effectively teach. You cannot distribute homework effectively per your stated dependence on these weekly parent reminders. Therefore I would like my child to be moved to another teacher immediately. I am totally disgusted with the management of the school as a whole

and I would like to request a meeting with the superintendent."

124

GIVE ME THE SAUSAGE

ANONYMOUS, FLORIDA

I TEACH EIGHTH GRADE ENGLISH, AND IT'S MY FIRST year. During my final period of the day, a female student walked into the classroom carrying a giant sausage. It was still wrapped and was called "Big Momma Sausage." I laughed a bit at the name but then forgot about it. While providing my direct instructions for the lesson, I heard a loud and persistent smacking sound. When I looked towards where the sound was coming from, the student was slapping another female student in the face with the sausage as she tried to swat it away.

My first instinct was to laugh because it was such a ridiculous thing to see, but I had to remind myself that I was the adult in the room. Therefore, I had to say the following sentence, which never in my entire life would I imagine I would have to say. I looked at a fourteen-year-old child in her eyes and said, "Your sausage privileges have been revoked for the entire class time. Please hand over the sausage. You will get it back at the end of the class!"

She wasn't happy about it but she did hand over the sausage. The class continued as usual until the bell rang.

The students left, and I was holding the door for them to exit, and we all forgot about the sausage on my desk. The student made it halfway down the hall when she suddenly remembered her forgotten sausage. She turned around and shouted across the hall, "Mister! GIVE ME THE SAUSAGE!" in front of the other teachers holding their doors and admin, who was monitoring the hallway. My eyes bugged out of my head, and I froze. But I quickly realized that I needed to show everyone that she was talking about an *actual* sausage.

I ran quickly into my room, grabbed the packed sausage, and held it high into the air while I ran back out to the hallway so that admin would understand and see what sausage my student was talking about. Having a fourteen-year-old child scream for me, her male teacher, to give her the sausage was not something they prepared me for in college.

PERSONAL NOTE

HOMEWORK ON GOOGLE CLASSROOM:

1. How does the system of checks and balances maintain separation of power and keep one branch from becoming too powerful?

Can you just take me out of this class? I'm not doing it anymore. I cry every time I look at this stupid google classroom and I don't care about the government so I'm not doing anything else in this class. I get this is like your whole life so I know you love it but I don't so I'm not filling my summer with it. You made this class start the same day as my other class so I wasn't finishing one before starting one so maybe next time this class won't make me want to cry and throw my computer at a wall. Just give me a zero if you have to. I'll be fine.

WELL THAT ESCALATED QUICKLY!

To: Woodrow's mother
From: Woodrow's teacher
Subject: Sustained absences

HELLO. WE HAVEN'T SEEN WOODY AT SCHOOL IN A while. I just wanted to make sure everything is OK. He can always arrange to make up work.

To: Woodrow's teacher
From: Woodrow's Mother
Subject: Re: Sustained absences

Hi. We have had a really hard time this year. Woody got bronchitis twice and then my husband had a car fall off a jack onto him and then my Uncle was being held in Mexico for ransom and two of his fingers were cut off and sent to us to let us know they were serious. So things have just been crazy.

A SMILE THAT DOESN'T WAVER

SHANNON, VIRGINIA

I HAD JUST RETURNED TO TEACHING AFTER TAKING A few years off to stay home with my children. My class was known as *the* class around the building. There were 24 students, which was unheard of in our tiny school system. Eleven were special ed., five were gifted, and three had severe behavior problems. Toss in a couple of crazy-ass parents, and it would have driven the best of teachers mad. I thought the year couldn't possibly get worse, and then I got the news that one of my fourth grade students was diagnosed with leukemia. She was the kindest of all children. She always had this smile that reached up to her ears and lit up the room. She was one of those rare kids that no one even had the heart to bully or pick on. She brought out the best in everyone. She had just lost her mother over the summer, and despite losing her mom and moving to a new state, she was the epitome of positivity.

Within two days of her diagnosis, she started chemotherapy and was put on homebound instruction. I couldn't fathom my day without this child in it, so despite already being stressed to the max with two small children of my own at home and this challenging class during the day, I signed up immediately. Every day after school, I'd head to her house. She'd be waiting for me on the couch every day with that bubbly smile on her face. There were days when she could barely lift her arm; she was so tired from treatments, and her hair began to fall out. Despite it all, her smile never wavered.

I was drowning in a sea of my own misery and negativity at the time, and this little girl saved me and my career. She had lost her mother, moved to a new state, was diagnosed with cancer, and lost her hair, yet she didn't complain. She studied hard, and she pushed through our lessons. Her courage and optimistic attitude so inspired me. How could my difficult year even begin to compare with what she had been through? The time I spent working one-on-one with her reminded me why I chose to teach.

The school I teach at only has a couple hundred children and 80% fall below the poverty line. Yet once word got out that this student had cancer, all the other students instantly wanted to help. They began a fundraiser, and the support was incredible. One child brought in her entire piggy bank she had been saving since she was born. Others turned in their ice cream money or allowances. They raised over $3,000, which, for a population that doesn't have much, was quite a feat. Her father was in tears when he was presented with the check.

I'm happy to say that she is currently in remission. She still faces two years of treatment to prevent the cancer from returning, yet she still always has that smile on her face. I think of her when I start feeling bad for myself about my circumstances, and I always find a new appreciation for what I have.

128

SORRY

To: English Teacher
From: Latrice your student
Subject: Sorry

I'M SORRY FOR BEING A BITCH IN CLASS AND NOT PAYING attention. I love you very much and you are my favorite teacher ever and you do a lot to help me out. Also some people in our class just aggravate me so much and need to be put in their place and that is why I yell at them when they piss me off. You are the queen of the class and we must respect you and love you and I need you because you are my best friend because you help me pass.

Have a dope weekend!

129

A TINY FUCKING HOUSE

ANONYMOUS

I WAS WORKING AT A MIDDLE SCHOOL WHERE MY BOSS was the most horrible person I've ever worked for. Nothing was ever the fault of the students, and she often made teachers cry. Working for her was absolute misery.

She was obsessed with winning awards. She actually spent money from our school budget to build a tiny house. Why would a public school need a tiny house next to it? Well, that would be to win an award.

This woman was all about winning awards. As part of the award process for a particular contest, they wanted an entire room dedicated to "evidence" that proved why the school should win. The principal decided since there wasn't an open room in the school that was not frequently in use, she would build a tiny house next to the building to put their evidence of greatness in. When she presented the idea to staff, some teachers literally left the meeting.

Nevertheless, the fucking tiny house got built, using the school's money. All of a sudden there wasn't enough money to purchase supplies for our classroom. Strange.

The school won the stupid award at the end of the year and the house disappeared over the summer. The fate of the tiny house is currently unknown. Hopefully someone burnt it to the ground.

The tiny fucking house

CREATIVE PARENTING DONE RIGHT

RACHEL GREENE, NEW HAMPSHIRE

I TEACH KINDERGARTEN AT AN INNER-CITY SCHOOL IN New Hampshire. One year I had a student who had never been to school and had just arrived here from another country. He was wild! He hit me, scratched me, ran away from me, etc. I expect a certain amount of this with kids who have never been to school, but this was next-level insane behavior! He ran around all day like a bat out of hell.

After a few days in school, I finally called the dad in for a meeting with my administrators. We laid it all on the table and said the behavior had to stop, or he would start receiving more severe consequences than losing recess time. The dad was so nice and apologetic and promised he would speak to his son about this, and the behavior would stop. After that day in September, the kid never acted up ever again. He was a completely different kid. I was in shock but so happy that his dad was able to remedy his son's behavior.

Fast forward to the end of November. The same dad came in for his parent conference.

Here is our conversation (one I will never forget):

Me: "So I noticed your son's behavior has really

changed. I so appreciate you speaking with him about it. Whatever you said really made an impact. Thank you so much."

Dad: "Well, haha! Yeah. You know how sometimes you have to lie to kids?"

Me: "Uh, yeah?"

Dad: "So the day we had the meeting, I came home and told his mother. We came up with a plan. We painted black and blue marks all over her face and body and ripped her clothes. We put bandages all over her with some fake blood and messed up her hair. When my son came home, his mom was sprawled out on a chair, moaning. He ran over to her, crying and wanted to know what happened. So we told him that when you are bad in school, a very bad man named Pepito comes and beats your mother."

Me: ...

I'm still speechless, but I applaud their creativity.

BOYS WILL BE BOYS AND OTHER HORSESHIT

J. MORRIS

IN MY LAST BOOK *MORE TEACHER MISERY*, I FOCUSED A lot on the lack of consequences for deplorable behavior in schools across the country. The most atrocious and often dangerous behavior is mostly ignored by administration because they are not allowed to actually punish kids anymore. I'd like to take a moment to focus on one specific aspect of this behavior that is widespread and somehow continues with no consequences: sexual harassment of teachers.

It is quite commonplace for a young, female teacher to be sexually harassed both verbally and physically by male students (and occasionally female students too). The general response to something that would absolutely be considered criminal behavior outside of school is "boys will be boys" and "deal with it." It is like being harassed is part of the job description, and if you complain too much about it, you are seen as a pain in the ass.

A Guardian U.K. article titled "From lewd comments to up-skirting: female teachers speak out about sexual harassment" describes the kind of sexual harassment that was allowed to go on in 2018. "There was one female member of staff... [pupils] found photos of her on Facebook and Photoshopped them with pictures of penises to make it look like she was giving someone a blowjob, printed them off, and cascaded them down the stairs. The head's reaction was to threaten to fire her. Nothing happened to the children." Can you imagine that? The administration actually tried to find fault with the teacher. If I were her, I'd be getting my files together for a big lawsuit, but the culture of fear at her workplace was too intimidating. At the same school, female staff who reported being sexually harassed by students saw no action taken. Another teacher "had her phone stolen by the kids, who rang her dad and said: 'We're going to rape your daughter outside school.' She wasn't supported by the school at all, and no one was interested."

In another situation, a group of students repeatedly called the school's main office posing as parents, and asked to be put through to a female teacher's extension. When she answered, the boys would make "really threatening, lewd comments. One kid said he was going to rape me; do it down my neck and into my face, or he was going to catch me later on my way to the train; he knew where I headed after school." She reported the situation to the principal, and she was told not to say anything because she might be "embarrassed" by the incident becoming public. She asked to involve the police and for the students to be held account- able, "But instead, the school simply shut down the internal telephone system."

"It becomes grinding," she said. "You have no idea what to do. You dread going in. In some classes, the boys would be so aggressive it would just be an hour of hell."

These stories are not uncommon. In the same article, a sociology teacher at a different school described how her fifteen-year-old male students asked her for blowjobs and made comments about her breasts in class. She felt too intimidated to report it to admin. "I hate to say it, but a lot of the time, I ignored it out of fear that it would somehow be seen to be my fault."

Another young English teacher said male students made "extremely sexually suggestive comments," and one repeatedly interrupted a lesson to ask her to be his valentine. "When I told him to stop as he was inappropriate," she said, "he told me he knew where I lived." When she reported this to administration, she was told to "adjust her teaching strategies and not tolerate his behavior." Another student said he "Wanted to anally fist her." When she reported it, not only was no action taken, but she was told to "expect" such harassment, and they said it "was normal boys' behavior."

This is very common in the U.S. as well. I will let the experiences of my followers speak for themselves. (Let me just add here that male teachers also get sexually harassed and other kinds of harassment also takes place, although I am choosing to focus on the prevalence of sexual harassment against female teachers by male students.)

"I work at an all-boys school. I was sexually assaulted by two students one day. I had to have personal meetings with them after their two-day suspension, and then they were back in my classroom. Apparently, there was a game the students were playing to see if they could get away with touching a teacher sexually."

"I worked at a school where kids were circulating upskirt pics of at least one female teacher. The kids got caught, but the consensus of staff and admin was that the teacher was asking for it, in a floor-length maxi skirt."

"A student sexually assaulted me, and when I went to

admin, I was the one who was under investigation to see if I had instigated it. I had never been more embarrassed and humiliated."

"I was sent porn links, threats of sexual violence (with graphic sexually violent images), and death threats by a student. Police were investigating, but one day into the investigation, the district asked me to transfer out of the school (I had been there for seven years) before police had concluded the investigation."

"I was only 24 when I started teaching. A 16-year-old boy who was way bigger than me blocked the door and wouldn't let me leave while two other kids stood in the hall and laughed. The boy was saying that I should ask him for permission to leave. It lasted at least 10 minutes. I cried on my way home. When I reported it the next day, the response I got was, 'Do you want him to be punished?' FUCK YES I DO! He got one day of in-school suspension and got removed from my class because *he* didn't feel comfortable."

"I was sent messages through our school's online message system from a male student with explicit sexual language about what he wanted to do to my butt. The school's police officer said it 'wasn't a threat,' so it wasn't a crime. Two of the three boys involved were removed from school by their parents, who didn't like that admin was considering punishing them. The kid who actually sent the message wasn't a student in my class, and since they couldn't 'prove' that he did it, there was no consequence for him."

"In my first year of teaching, I taught a credit recovery class for second semester seniors who had failed. They were mostly male and eighteen years old. They would blast porn from their phones, talk about gang-raping me, make sexual comments about me, etc. I documented everything and sent email after email. Admin, of course, did nothing. The only threat the boys received was that they would potentially lose prom. They didn't."

"A former student of mine played porn in class. The admin said that they would do something about it, but the student continued making sexual comments towards me. I reported it because I didn't want my other students to think that it was okay to speak that way. Again, nothing was done."

"A middle school student groped a female teacher and his punishment was to hand out pencils at an awards assembly. He was back in her classroom the next day."

"I received an incredibly lewd email from a student that is so inappropriate I don't even feel comfortable sharing what it said. I just couldn't believe the sexual things he said about my body. The issue made it up to the district level, but there was never a real punishment."

"A male student gave me his cellphone number and told me to call him if I was ever alone with a particular student who sat across from him. He didn't want me to be alone with him because he made lewd comments about me that were so offensive one girl who overheard it couldn't even repeat it. I reported this to admin and the female student had to write down what she heard. It matched the accounts that two other students gave. Admin said, 'Well, you're a young, pretty girl. You should expect it.' He went on to say how sometimes my clothes seemed too tight or too short, and the female administrator said, 'Stand up. Let's see what you're wearing today.' I was humiliated. The student was moved from my class, but there was no further punishment. A male teacher asked why I was making the student's life so much harder and added that nothing terrible had *actually* happened to me."

"I received death threats, and a threatening email the district refused to track. I was scared for my life, but blamed for not 'trying harder with struggling learners.'"

"My district recently took rape off the discipline matrix as a zero-tolerance offense."

"A student sexually harassed me, and when I reported it, I was told by admin, two weeks later, that the student 'wouldn't even remember what he said' and that it wasn't a big deal."

"In my first year out of undergrad, I taught at a technical college, so my students were mostly male, and all were adults. I had one student whose first language was Spanish, so sometimes he'd stay after class and I'd help him by summarizing the lesson for him in Spanish and doing some practice problems on the board. This lasted no more than five minutes. Well, apparently, he took that as me flirting and starting leaving notes on my desk about how beautiful I was and that he loved me. I kept all the notes and reported it to my boss, but nothing was done. Then, the student started closing and locking the door during these sessions. I reported that. When he stuck out his arms and physically blocked me between the wall and my desk and began telling me how beautiful I was, I went into fight or flight mode and pushed past him and went immediately to my boss to say I was uncomfortable. Several days later, I was called into a 'mediation meeting' with H.R., my boss, and the student, where I was told the relationship wasn't inappropriate since the student was at the college level. There were no rules against student-teacher relationships. I was told that if I didn't want to encourage the student, I should insist on taking our after-class conversations to the hallway. I didn't continue my contract with that school the next year."

"I had a group of 7th grade boys who would make sexual moaning noises any time they saw me. When I reported it to the principal, the response I got was, 'boys will be boys.' The next year one of these boys got my phone number somehow and began sending me messages asking me to wear a short skirt to school, send him nude photos, etc. I reported it to admin and he got no consequence because he cried when he was confronted about it. They said they felt his embarrassment for being caught was enough punishment."

"In my first year of teaching, I had a male student continually make inappropriate comments and always try to touch me (forced hugs, hand on my waist, leaning on me in the hallway). I told the office about it several times, and their response was, 'You need to get better at redirecting his attention.' It got so bad that I asked the male teachers across the hall from me to check in periodically to make sure I didn't need help. One of the teachers who was also the student's football coach responded, 'Oh, that's just Mike!' Like oh, okay! I didn't realize he was special!"

"When I first started teaching, I would always wear nice knee-length dresses and cardigans and other cute professional elementary art teacher outfits. A group of 6th grade boys was caught calling me hot and sexy. What did my school do? They told me I needed to wear clothes that covered more and stop dressing up. Thanks! I'll wear yoga pants and an oversized t-shirt from now on, and feel completely ashamed and disgusted with my body as a bonus."

"I was called a 'fucking dyke' by a student. The district told me to counsel him on sexual harassment."

"A student once told me there was a picture of my butt circulating on Snapchat. When I asked security to look into it, they laughed and said they'd like to see that picture too."

"Students comment on my body, my big butt, and generally demean my figure regularly. I told admin about it and they said, 'Oh, you're young!'"

"When I taught grade eight, one student said, 'I want to cover you in chocolate sauce, and rage fuck you.' He never got in trouble."

"I taught at an all-boys catholic school in a major U.S. city. Students called me 'sweet tits' in the hallway and put their hands up my skirt. I had a student bait me so the other one could take a picture up my skirt with their cell phone camera. I was humiliated. I went to our all-male administration, and nothing was done. Our vice principal, who was a state senator, told me to stop wearing skirts. I had to get the police involved because they refused to expel the kid."

"I had a male student lean down in his desk and take several photos on his phone under my long skirt. I deleted all the photos on his phone and his iPod. When I reported him to the male assistant principal I was told, 'It's the last day of school, and he is basically graduated, so just let it go.' He walked at graduation and had no consequences."

"I had a boy secretly take a picture of me and Photoshop it with a penis by my mouth and then spread it via social media. Admin made him apologize to me. Of course, he was kept in my class. When I told my husband about the situation, he wanted to go to my school and beat up admin and I had to beg him not to, so I could keep my job. At that point I was stuck—I had something like fifteen years at this school. My income is necessary for my family of four to get by."

"I am a physical education teacher, and one of my coworkers had an 8th grade boy expose himself to her, and her administration did NOTHING. I had just started teaching, and I received a lot of unwanted attention. Boys whistled and made inappropriate comments, and then a boy asked me for my number, and I lost it. I went to the head of discipline and told him, and he replied precisely, 'Do you think I can do something about it every time a child comments like that? No. So deal with it.'"

"I had my butt touched on a few separate occasions. I reported it from day one, and the 7th grade boy was first just asked to apologize. When it got to grabbing, I called the mom for a meeting. She showed up with her sister, who works as a teacher in the same district and started yelling at me and accusing me of being racist."

"When I was still in grad school, and in my student teaching experience in an autism support classroom, a middle school student started touching himself inappropriately under the table while I was teaching his small group. I couldn't see what he was doing from my angle, but my mentor teacher was watching from a few feet away. She called me over to talk to me about how my outfit (a cowl-neck sweater, in case you were wondering) was not appropriate while teaching middle school boys. Instead of using it as a teachable moment for the student about how this is not an appropriate behavior in school, she blamed me."

"During my first year teaching, I had a fourth grader pull my arms behind my back, dry hump me and say he wanted to 'chain me up.' The principal's only consequence was a loss of one recess."

"I had a student who constantly sexually harassed me throughout an entire school year. He would air hump in my direction. He left me notes, saying, 'I want to fuck you in the asshole.' He called me a bitch, cunt, and yelled out, 'suck my dick' a lot in class. He once whispered, 'I want you to have my baby' into my ear. I reported the behavior over and over to admin, the school psychologist, his counselor, and even H.R. No one cared. They scheduled a meeting with his mom without me, even though I thought it was very important that I be in that meeting. The next day he said to me, 'You better watch your back because I will find you and kill you.' When I reported that, the consequence was that he couldn't come to my class for two days. When he returned, the abuse continued. I asked my union rep. for help, and she laughed at me. She said that a student had actually tried to kill her while she hid in a closet. 'Harassment is a rite of passage for female teachers,' she said. 'One day, you will laugh at this.' Years later, I'm not laughing."

"An eighth grade student full-on grabbed my butt and squeezed it three times. I reported it to admin but the student denied it and admin said, 'He's a really good kid. I'm sure he didn't mean to. He's really upset. You should apologize for accusing him of that.' He faced no consequences, and a month later, he did the same thing to another female teacher."

"Two male students in my fifth grade class started a contest to see who could grab my butt as I walked by without getting caught. They told other kids, and I was grabbed continuously in the hallway. Admin gave them one detention and told me to stop wearing dresses and only to wear pants."

MORNING COCKTAIL

ANONYMOUS

I TEACH EIGHTH GRADE ENGLISH AND RECENTLY GOT A new student. His name is Seven. Now that's not his real name, but his gang name. He proudly shared that with the class and showed us his very real and quite large arm tattoo of that name, which he got in prison. This kid is only 15 years old by the way.

Each day Seven rolled up late to school around 10 AM and reeked of weed. Usually, he just wandered the hallways looking lost, but on this day he decided to join our class.

Seven walked in, sat down, said, "Sup bitch," to his friend, and then pulled out lemonade and a bottle of unlabeled cough syrup. He then proceeded to pour the cough syrup into the lemonade and make lean in the middle of class.[1] The entire class, including me, stared in complete shock. Seven took a swig of his morning cocktail.

I finally told him to get out of the classroom. I called the nurse, the office, and all emergency numbers. Seven walked down the hallway and out of the building, screaming that I was a "fucking rat." No one stopped him.

He showed up outside my room a few hours later like

nothing had happened. I called admin again and it took them 30 minutes to get him out of the hallway because he refused to leave. He was suspended for two weeks and then appeared back in my class once again, with a creepy smile on his face.

SHIT IN THE LUNCH BUCKET

ANONYMOUS

OUR LOVELY SCHOOL (WHICH HAS NO FUNDING TO HEAT the outhouse-style bathrooms in the winter) is lucky enough to have a plasma TV, Apple TV, and iPad in each of its portable classrooms. But over Christmas break, a man quickly stole several of them from numerous classrooms in broad daylight, on two separate thieving sprees. Students and staff returned in January to a school with boarded-up windows and no word from admin regarding these thefts or improved security measures to prevent further damage.

Fast forward to MLK weekend. On Sunday, I received an email stating that, yet again, our school was broken in to. This time my classroom had been hit. I was told to report to school on my day off to clean up the overturned classroom. I was greeted by a temporary security guard, who I had implored my principal to hire permanently, considering I weigh 108 pounds and would have no defense if the thief decided to return for a fourth helping of public school goods.

"Wow, wow, wow, wow," the security guard stated with no hint of surprise in his voice as he followed me into the classroom. "See, I'm onto this guy," he continued as I gave him the stink eye. "This guy wants me to think there's a bunch of them working together. But no! There's just one burglar. See, I found only one set of footprints out back, so I know it was only one guy."

"Well, gee Mr. Holmes," I thought. "I'm so glad it's still 1892, and footprints are the only clue we have to solve a crime."

I spent the next two hours turning desks back over, cleaning up the work that had been ripped off the wall, and making a list of both personal and school items which had been stolen. When the classroom finally looked somewhat normal–save for the boarded up windows and shattered glass that hid in every nook and cranny of the room–I went home.

The next day, I returned to school, ready to discuss the crime with my students. However, upon their arrival, it only took a few minutes to find one last present the thief had left behind. As they unpacked their things for the day, one unsuspecting child headed over to our class lunch bucket–a repurposed storage tub that had been beautifully decorated by the proud students of Room 13. Students put their lunches in this bucket every morning before they started their school day. The moment she lifted the lid, the room was filled with the most unbelievable stench. Initially, I assumed one notorious student had let one rip. But no, this morning he was not to blame.

"Um," the girl said hesitantly, "I need to show you something." She ushered me over and opened the bucket. Not only was I assailed yet again by the deadly odor– directly in my face this time since I had bent down to see what she was looking at–but I saw with my own eyes a massive pile of human shit at the depths of our beloved lunch bucket. Quickly realizing the mayhem that would no doubt ensue, I said to her, "Tell *no one*," and placed the shit bucket outside for the janitor to haul away.

Despite my efforts, it was too late. In the minute it took for me to stare at that pile of shit and realize what atrocity had been committed, the students could already smell it. Each student who arrived that day took one sniff and quickly shoved their nose into their shirt collar.

Normally, when a student passes gas, I tell the kids to get over it, it isn't that bad, and it'll go away in a minute. Not today. It was so wretched that I had a strong urge to open the windows, only to remember that we no longer had windows. The stink was so unavoidably horrid that I had to evacuate my entire class to a neighboring classroom until it aired out.

As luck would have it, the school board happened to be visiting that day, and not only was I waiting for them to stumble upon my empty, shit-filled classroom, but my principal was conveniently unreachable since the day prior, despite various calls and emails. I knew I had to get ahead of this before the kids went home to tell their parents, who would undoubtedly throw an overdramatic fit and attempt to file a public health claim against the school. Eventually, within the last twenty minutes of the school day, I finally reached the principal and explained to her that not only had all of our technology been stolen and our windows broken, but the thief also took a dump in our lunch bucket. I expressed my concern that their parents would be contacting me about this.

Here is the advice I received from the fearless leader of our fine school: "Just tell the kids to be optimistic! We need to carry on as if nothing has happened. Don't tell the parents anything in detail. Just say that we were broken into, and nothing more. Remember, *be optimistic!*"

OPTIMISTIC!? Our belongings had been stolen, the classroom was destroyed, and there were human feces where the lunches were supposed to go, but I'm going to look on the bright side of things—at least it wasn't diarrhea!

Several days later, I made a massive stink (pun intended) regarding our school's security. Their only response was to install more security cameras. So now we can watch the fecal bandit coming and going from five different angles, and there's a zoom feature! Yet we won't be alerted in real-time of these midday break-ins, nor will there be any preventative measures taken to avoid them.

YOU TEACHERS ARE LIKE PERSONAL ASSISTANTS, RIGHT?

From: Parent of student you had last year
Subject: Walmart
Date: July 4, 2019, 2:25 PM

HOPE THIS FINDS YOU WELL. CAN YOU PLEASE HELP ME get Walmart gift cards from any Walmart store in the area, I need to send them as birthday gifts for loved ones, I can't pick them up myself as I am on a trip. Please put them in my mailbox and I'll repay you when I get home.

WHY NO ONE WANTS TO BE PEP SQUAD ADVISOR

ANONYMOUS

As a new teacher who was desperate for a job, I eagerly agreed to be Pep Squad advisor for 60 girls in addition to the attached teaching gig.

The woman who previously held this title, I would find out later, had a mental breakdown in the middle of the year and had to go on medical leave. After I gained tenure and left the position as pep squad advisor, the athletic director had to take over the job because they could not convince any teacher to take on the role.

I had a nice parent as an assistant advisor who showed me the ropes, and I felt confident that I could change some policies and start to deal with some of the prevalent behavioral issues that were embedded in the cheer culture at my school.

One of the policies I decided to take on was the lack of consequences for poor behavior. Previously, girls earned "demerits" if they were late, disrespectful, didn't dress appropriately, etc. Disrespect, in particular, had become a problem, and the demerits were not working. It was sometimes difficult to retain coaches willing to work part-time, for little pay. Working with the parent advisor and coaches, the new consequence for disrespect and tardiness was to be benched at the next game. We figured no one would ever be late. On the morning we were set to leave for cheer camp, eight girls were 20-40 minutes late to the bus, and we were late to camp. Under this new contract (which all the girls and their parents signed), I was forced to bench them for the first football game.

Parent meetings ensued, first with the athletic director and then with the principal. Each time my administration backed up my decision. The moms were not happy that they could not get their way by being the squeaky wheel, so they took it to the next level.

As I stood on the sidelines at our first home football game, I could hear students chanting, "Let them cheer!" As I turned to look at the student section, I saw students holding signs that read, "Let them cheer!" I could see the two moms I had tangled with in meetings that week, handing out the signs. Students I knew and loved were protesting against me. I was mortified. My principal ignored it, citing free speech. Other teachers on the sidelines were flabbergasted; a couple of them felt for me and went up into the stands to collect as many signs as they could. Another teacher asked some of the kids if they even knew what they were protesting and that they were upsetting me. They said they had no idea – they were just following along. This continued the entire game, as I had to put on a front that everything was fine, and continue to supervise the girls as if nothing was wrong. Meanwhile, half of the girls who were benched smirked on the sidelines, feeling vindicated.

As I walked out of the stadium that night, my husband holding my hand because he knew how upset I was, I was heckled by two moms. They walked behind us the whole way, loudly discussing what a lousy role model I was.

Soon after, a mom sent me an email, cc'd to the principal, alleging that I had ruined her daughter's dreams of becoming a history teacher. A few of her daughter's friends told me that she was high at cheer practice. They were worried about her. She was lifting girls into the air while high, which was very dangerous. I turned her in, hoping she would get help. The school's police officer found drugs on her, so she was served with a ticket and had to go to court. I had grounds to kick her off the team for this but decided that being on the team would keep her out of more trouble. Her punishment/requirement to stay on the team was to come in on the weekend and help the coaches steam clean the mats. Her mom felt that this punishment was too extreme and that I had no right to contact the police officer about her. She said that her daughter looked up to me, and felt betrayed and angry towards teachers in general, and no longer wanted to be a teacher.

Later that year, another mom tried to have me fired after I benched her daughter a second time for calling the coach a "bitch" during a game. She took her complaints to the district office, and a private investigator was hired to be impartial in the investigation. I was completely exonerated, but the stress took a toll on my marriage and my health. Years later, I'm still teaching, but the stress of that experience has left its mark.

136

IRRESPONSIBLE

To: Barf's Teacher
From: Barf's Mom
Subject: Doctor's apt.

HELLO. MY SON HAS A DOCTOR'S APPOINTMENT AT
9:15 tomorrow morning. Please don't forget!

To: Barf's mom
From: Barf's Teacher
Subject: Re: Doctor's apt.

No problem! The absence will be excused as
long as he brings a note. Have a great day!

To: Barf's Teacher
From: Barf's Mom
Subject: Re: Re: Doctor's apt.

YOU FORGOT TO TAKE BARF TO HIS DOCTOR'S APPOINTMENT THIS MORNING! I REMINDED YOU SEVERAL TIMES! THIS IS SO IRRESPONSIBLE!

137

PARENTS WHO OVERSHARE

J. MORRIS

I DON'T KNOW WHAT IT IS ABOUT TEACHERS THAT MAKE parents feel so damn comfortable, but they say some weird shit to us! Maybe it's because we can't say anything inappropriate back? Just check out these ridiculous comments that have been made to teachers:

A 62-year-old father of 12 children: "You don't need to worry about job security because I have plenty more seed in me!"

"My son's behavioral issues are related to his undescended testicle."

A mom who came in to pick up her high-as-a-kite son (who got suspended), proceeded to tell the whole office staff, "He ain't no man! He still leaves shit stains in his underwear!"

"My son isn't sleeping well because he is up all night watching porn."

"My son just started to grow hair down there."

A fifth grade boy had missed the first few days of school. The dad escorted him into class on his first day back in the middle of a lesson. In front of the whole class, the dad said,

"I apologize for my son's absence. He was just circumcised."

As the teacher was trying to get into her car to leave after back to school night, a mom followed her and said, "I didn't graduate from high school and instead had my first kid. I used to do a lot of drugs and party, which is where my first two kids came from. My next two kids came from one-night stands."

"I'm on my period, that's why my son has been crying."

"Could you talk to my son about going in my closet and borrowing from my collection of porn? Maybe he'll listen to you."

Holding out a tissue full of mucus a mom comments, "This is mostly clear, so I think he can stay at school. What do you think?"

"I have five kids because my method is to keep my legs closed, but as you can see, that's clearly not working out for me."

"I put the wrong email on the parent contact form. That's the email where I get all my porn messages."

"My son is not a drug baby, even though I was doing drugs while I was pregnant."

"When do the students learn about sex ed. because my son is always touching himself!"

"I couldn't get my son to school yesterday because I had a very serious interaction between my blood pressure meds and my Viagra."

"My son has to wear the baggy pants low because his testicles are extremely large."

Teacher: "Your granddaughter has been talking excessively in class."
Grandma: "It's puberty. My mother shaved my pubic region

after I started my period, and I'm still smooth as ever down there at 60 years old!"

"One of my son's testicles is a lot bigger than the other."

Pregnant mom to the teacher before conference: "Do you have a pillow I can sit on? I have nasty hemorrhoids."

"I just had a vasectomy. Do you want some free advice? Don't ever get married."

"My daughter complains of her breast buds hurting. Can you recommend a cream or lotion for that?"

"You know we still co-sleep because of his seizures. None of us slept very well last night, because he would not stop masturbating between his father and me!"

"My daughter's breasts are going to be huge because all the women in our family have some big old thangs!"

"My son gets uncomfortable because his scrotum sticks to his leg in this heat."

"My daughter has a ton of bras, but she wears the same one every day, and she never washes it!"

"If you want to get pregnant, you should sit against the wall with your legs up after having sex."

"My daughter was miraculously conceived."

"My daughter got her period, and we took her to the hospital. They put her on the pill, but she's not sexually active. Her hymen is still intact. Could you remind her to take her pill every day?"

"I'm pregnant too, but I'm going to have it taken care of later today."

"In our house, we refer to her privates as her flower pot."

What It's Really Like

138

A SOPPING WET SURPRISE

ANONYMOUS

I was fresh out of the local college's teacher education program with a shiny new degree and still flying high from a solid student teaching experience. Halfway through the fall semester of my first year, my third block of students and I had come to a hard-fought yet cautious understanding, and as this is a book for teachers, let this description suffice: *They were freshmen.*

It was a Monday, because *of course it was.* A few minutes before the bell, the students were pouring through the door to my classroom—loud, jostling, shoving, and really just enjoying being 15 years old. A quiet boy, we'll call him Leroy, came up to my desk as the class began to settle in.

"Mr. D-"

"Yeah, Leroy. What's up?"

"I found something on the floor."

"What is it?" He had his hand cupped as he extended it to me. "I dunno; I think it's drugs." I looked down at the bright orange pill in his palm. "Okay, give it here, go sit down. Thanks for turning it in."

As he went back to his desk and the two-minute bell

sounded, I took a closer look at the pill. "U30" was printed on one side. I Googled it and sure enough it was Adderall, a schedule II amphetamine. The kids who had a script for ADD would sometimes sell hits of it to their classmates who would chop it up and snort it. It wasn't a particularly big deal because we were having a pill problem that year with our students, but I still needed to turn it in. I looked at my watch and there were maybe another ninety seconds till the tardy bell. I figured I'd put it in a plastic bag, run it to the SRO and let him deal with it. I'd get back in time to teach these kids *The Odyssey*.

I know some of you are judging me right now. *Never leave your class.* I know. I get it. They tell us this in teacher prep programs, and admin tells us time and again, "Don't ever leave your room." And you would think after that first month of trying to teach *Lord of the Flies* to a gaggle of pubescent psychos, I would have known better than to leave them to their own devices, even for less than three minutes.

I was young. It was my first year.

Officer M. was a jolly soul who loved to swap stories. In another life, he would have made an incredible teacher, but he chose to be a cop. On the way to his office, I started to think it might not be as swift of an exchange as I thought. "Here's the drugs. I gotta go," I said in haste. By the way, that wouldn't have been a bad senior motto for this class.

The tardy bell rang while I was still in Officer M's office. He was ribbing me for turning it in. "Man, why didn't you just eat it right there in front of him?" I enjoyed his company; it was always warm and irreverent in a place that's often very cold and takes itself just a little too seriously. "Officer, I have to get back. I've got a class waiting on me."

On the way back to the room, as I got closer to the open

door, that familiar, dull roar of teenagers being social and the sound of metal chairs scooting over a waxed floor was absent. An eerie, total silence ushered me into my classroom. It was dead quiet, not even a nervous giggle. I should have delayed the lesson and confronted the vibe; if it had occurred now, ten years later, I would know the bastards were plotting something. But, never one to look a gift horse in the mouth, I interpreted this solemn quiet as respect in anticipation of my meticulously prepared lesson. I told them all to get their books out and turn to the appropriate page number while I moved to the board to write out additional instructions.

And then I saw it.

Right there, stuck square in the middle of my whiteboard, held on by a hastily-applied strip of scotch tape, glaring me in the face, was a sopping-wet, used tampon.

Apparently the Adderall found on the floor had belonged to one of my precious young female scholars, and she had not taken kindly to my delivering her product to the fuzz. Her displeasure was glistening red under that soft fluorescent light.

When the class saw whatever expression came across my face in that terrible moment, the room went wild, all 35 of them broke into fits of laughter as I stood there stunned and confused.

Then came my second potentially career ending offense of the day. Having discarded hygiene products stuck to your stuff tends to bring out the worst in people (or so I've heard). I felt the word erupting up from the core of my being like vomit, and I knew I wasn't going to be able to stop it.

With all the jadedness and frustration of every teacher who has had to deal with this kind of bullshit since the beginning, I shouted over them all, "Are you *fucking* kidding me???"

There was a collective gasp, a shocked silence, and then a stillness fell over them so I could repeat the word in case they hadn't felt it the first time. "Are you *fucking* serious!?" It was loud enough for every teacher in the hallway to peek a head out the door and wonder who had finally cracked. I said it, and it felt good and right, and in that moment, I didn't care how this would reflect on my End of Year professionalism rubric. Mentally, I just added it to the growing list of things I wish I could tell my principal to shove up his ass.

At that point, I was ready to clean out my desk and turn in my badge, but before I left, somebody was going to pay for this. You can't stick used tampons on your teacher's whiteboard and get away with it. So I went to my desk with the class still sitting in stunned silence, unsure of what to do next. I opened a drawer and pulled out the first-aid kit we're required to keep in the room. I pulled on a pair of rubber gloves, went to the board, peeled off the tampon, and threw it into an empty Band-Aid box.

I took the box and stormed out of the room towards my grade-level admin's office. I didn't know what the protocol was for smeared menstrual blood on school property, but I intended to find out. I went to his office, slammed the door behind me, and set the box on his desk.

"Look what they put on my white board!"

He opened the box and calmly replied, "Classy." I didn't understand why he didn't share my outrage. I guess you had to be there.

"What are you going to do about this?" I yelled.

"Mr. D., you need to calm down."

The rest of the conversation isn't worth transcribing. I kept my job. Apparently, after a lot of stern lecture, the school felt the F-bomb was warranted in this extremely rare occurrence, but I was warned to never do it again.

In a reasonable world, a teacher could step out of his or her class for 60 seconds to use the bathroom. In a sensible world, you'd think we could trust 35 teenagers to refrain from fighting and ransacking the classroom while you pee. But this isn't a rational or reasonable world. This is a world where they shove 35 fifteen-year-olds in a single class and still report a 15:1 student-faculty ratio. This is public education, where insanity is the norm, and take it from me: *You better piss your pants before you take your eye off those kids.*

The student who did it got caught, by the way. She received half a day of in-school suspension.

THIS PARK AIN'T FOR PUNKS!

Weather Policies

(What is going to happen if there is a severe thunderstorm? A tornado warning? Light rain? Will your park remain open or closed? Describe your policy below:)

My MOMMa
aiht raised
no bitch

MAKE ROOM FOR THAT!

From: Moltar's mom
To: Moltar's computer science teacher
Subject: Moltar's skills

HELLO,

I am Moltar's mother. I know that Moltar's computer science skills race beyond his classroom perception because I see the work he creates outside class and it is mind-boggling to me. Something happened to his grade in your class that doesn't seem to make any sense. If you would like to see some of the work he does on his own time in order to raise his grade please make room for that in your grade book. I understand that you have a lot of students but my son is special in your course and deserves recognition for that, not a bad grade. Please spend the time to re-review his grades and see the work he does outside of class. I am hoping that all of the missing assignments he has missed won't affect his grade that much.

Please consider!

WHAT IS TEACHING REALLY LIKE?

KAREN JEFFRIES (@HILARIOUSLY_INFERTILE)

"After 30 years of doing such work, I have concluded that classroom teaching... is perhaps the most complex, most challenging, and most demanding, subtle, nuanced, and frightening activity that our species has ever invented. The only time a physician could possibly encounter a situation of comparable complexity would be in the emergency room of a hospital during or after a natural disaster."

Lee Shulman, *The Wisdom of Practice*

THE PROFESSION OF TEACHING, SPECIFICALLY elementary education, is mostly populated by females, and primarily, but not completely, female mothers. This gender dominance should not be lost on anyone. Teachers act as parents to their students, and all parents are teachers for their children. It doesn't matter if a parent has an MBA or never finished their GED, parents are perpetually teaching their children, whether they realize it or not. But what happens when the parents aren't actually *trying* to teach their children anything of use? What happens when some of the parents were never taught the basics of life, including self-care and hygiene, and the more significant parts of life, like how to love others? How do their children learn those skills? That is what I often face in my fourth grade dual language (Spanish/English) classroom outside New York City.

My students come to me at 8:24 in the morning with truckloads of baggage that I am acutely sensitive to while, at the same time, try not to bring attention to. Many of my students come from loving homes, where the parents are excellent teachers. Some of my students come from homes with domestic violence, drugs, and alcohol, all at their fingertips.

One of my students struggles to get her homework completed because her parents are fighting in their one-bedroom apartment, and she hides in the bathroom to escape the fury of their anger. Another one of my students, who is cognitively low-functioning, is punished by her parents who force her to kneel on rice for hours at a time because she struggles to add simple one-digit addition in fourth grade. One student cannot read on a first-grade level, his parents are illiterate in their native language, and from all observations and records over the years, they show their child very little love and affection. Another student comes from a home with lots of love and affection but came to school this year with a desire to kill himself, and a plan to make his wish a reality. Countless students over the years come to school with their fingernails black with dirt, their teeth not brushed, and their clothes not clean.

During a parent conference when I was teaching first grade, a father was so intoxicated that he fell asleep or passed out during the meeting. When he regained consciousness, we ended the meeting. My classroom reeked of alcohol, so much so that I was scared the next parent to enter the room would think that I had been drinking, so I sprayed the room with lemon-scented Lysol to mask the remaining musk of the previous father. I fondly remember that student very well. Every project that we assigned came back constructed out of alcohol bottle caps, beer bottle tops, and wine corks. The geometry project, where students were to find different 3D shapes in their houses, identify them, and make a creation out of them—were all alcohol containers. For the Hundredth Day of School project, where students need to count 100 items and glue them to a poster board in some creative fashion, his were made of beer bottle caps and corks, again. This student was smart and had massive potential, and when his parents picked him up from school they walked four feet in front of him the whole way home.

I taught three brothers from the same family, a few years apart. They struggled financially so badly, that they only had enough money to heat one bathtub full of hot water, once a week. The youngest brother was allowed to bathe after the rest of the family, in cold, dirty bathwater. Despite his home life, each day he came to my classroom with the best smile on his face, ready to read and learn in two languages.

Three out of five weekday mornings one of my students would come to school early for extra help. We would sit in a small group and work on simple sentences. Very quickly, I realized that his teeth weren't brushed, *ever*. When I asked him about it, he told me he did brush his teeth, but a simple smile said otherwise. I bought him a children's toothbrush and his choice of toothpaste and showed him the special place that we were going to keep it in the classroom. Then I watched from the other side of the room as he "brushed" his teeth, in a way that suggested that no one in his life had ever taught him how to brush his teeth before. In private, we worked together on the proper way to brush. He came to school every day and happily brushed his teeth in my classroom sink until the last day of school.

After her little sister was born, one of my students refused to eat solid food. She would only drink her food, like the baby. I had to work with her mother to, little by little, get her daughter back onto solid foods again in first grade.

Another first-grade student would perpetually place her hands in between her legs and rock back and forth. She was the sweetest, cutest, smartest kid ever, but when she got nervous, she would put her hands in between her legs, over her clothes, and rock to calm herself down. When we were in small group instruction, I had to make a point to tell all the students that we were going to keep our hands on the table. She would try to lower her hands and needed constant reminders to keep her hands on the table.

This is the reality of teaching in 2020. It isn't all dark stories of hard times. There are many amazingly positive moments of light, breakthroughs, and achievement, but there are so many parts of teaching that no one talks about, the parts that don't fit into the cells of a spreadsheet. This is the part of teaching that when you hear your brand new superintendent tell the staff on opening day that, "Some data looks good, but some data shows areas of much-needed improvement," you want to scream and storm out because you don't care if Juan from your class passes the state test, you care that he is alive in May to even take the test.

We are responsible for teaching children the standards of our specific grade level, measures that were developed by people who have little to no teaching experience, and even less understanding of child development. We parent our students for the eight hours of the day that we see them. We teach them right from wrong and just from unjust, in a world that may or may not have shown them justice in their short lives. We must bring light and positivity for them when, often, their candle burned out long ago, even for elementary students. We must accept them where they are academically, while gently pushing them to limits that their brains cannot yet reach. We answer to administration when they ask us about student progress, and *their* administration when they ask about test scores. We are ridiculed about state tests when we are trying with all our might to keep students clean, healthy, safe, cared for, and sadly, sometimes we are just trying to keep them alive.

142

FUNNY YOU SHOULD MENTION THE WORD UNCOMFORTABLE

Good Morning,
Just a FYI - I'd decided not to let ▰▰▰
wear his pj's today because it is really
cold today and he isn't able to control
his "manhood" (smile). Wearing pj's
will allow his "manhood" to be noticed
if he becomes excited; therefore, I did
not want anyone (including himself)
feel uncomfortable or embarrassed.

Have great day!

143

PINK CAR

EMILY NOLAN, VIRGINIA

I WAS 22, HAD JUST GRADUATED COLLEGE AND I WAS IN grad school at night. I was supposed to be student teaching all day for my Master's, but the school I was assigned to had recently lost 22 teachers the year before due to budget cuts and lack of pay raises. So I showed up the week before school, and they said, "Since you have a bachelor's degree, we're going to use you this year as an actual teacher and just count it as your student teaching."

I was young, and in no position to pass up getting paid for my credits. So I agreed to teach third grade with zero training. On the first day, I was approached by a second-grade teacher who wanted to warn me about a particular student in my class. Her exact words were, "You have Pink Car. She's a handful. Keep an eye on her at all times." Pink Car? I was confused but just nodded my head and thanked her for the head's up.

Handful doesn't even *begin* to describe this child. She had an alter ego, which was a car and she liked to be referred to as "Ms. Pink Car." She would "drive" around my room frequently, run out of gas, and would refuse to move.

Sometimes her "brakes" would give out, and she'd run around the school like a crazy person while we tried to "fix the brakes."

One day she was in a small group with five other students when another student called her by her real name instead of Ms. Pink Car. I could see the rage build up inside her and I knew something was going to happen, I just couldn't predict what.

Very quickly she grabbed a pencil and stabbed this little boy directly in the forehead with it. Shocked and panicked, I had my assistant bring the little boy to the nurse and got the rest of my class out into the hallway. Ms. Pink Car then went on a destructive rampage. She threw desks, chairs, and computers, and knocked over bookshelves while screaming, *"I'm Ms. Pink Car!"*

As a first year teacher who was really an unlicensed *student* teacher, I had absolutely no clue what to do. They definitely don't teach you how to handle situations like this in college, and I wasn't trained in how to restrain a student at the time, so that was totally out of the question. I called for my principal, who responded with, "I just sat down to eat lunch. Can it wait?" I politely responded with, "Absolutely not, you need to get here *now!*"

Ms. Pink Car and the principal did not have a good relationship because, as you can imagine, she was in his office quite frequently. The minute he stepped foot in my classroom, he just fueled her rage. She climbed up on a table and removed every single piece of her clothing. Then she turned around, bent over, exposed her entire rear end to us and yelled, "Get a load of my *asshole*, you fucking idiots!"

I was sort of laughing and crying at the same time. The principal, who had been in education for 20+ years compared to my whole seven weeks of experience said,

"What do you think we should do?" I said I think we needed to wait her out. We waited and watched as she continued her meltdown, and within minutes she was exhausted and collapsed onto the floor. It was almost like she had blacked out. She said she didn't remember anything that had happened.

We had several issues with her for the remainder of the year. The principal would "suspend" her for a few days, which did absolutely nothing. I reached out to district child psychologists and social workers, and she was put on a behavior plan that worked about 40% of the time. There was more violence, behavior disruptions, threats, and even hallucinations throughout the year. The school psychologist swore there was nothing wrong with her. This was mainly because she was smart enough to know when someone was observing her, and of course, she would act like a perfect angel then.

I sobbed on the phone to my mother on my way home from work that day, telling her this was the worst profession ever, and I couldn't do it. But I woke up the next day and went to work. Like all teachers, we have awful days that we could never have imagined, but we still teach. We still show up for the kids. And thankfully, although my teaching experiences have always been challenging, I have never had an experience quite like Ms. Pink Car again.

144

MOM NEEDS A DICTIONARY

Hello

I don't think it's appropriate that you teach about homophones at this young age. I would prefer that ~~████~~ be excluded from class discussion at that time.

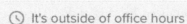

🕐 It's outside of office hours

145

RAW COCONUTS

KRISTEN, SOUTH FLORIDA

I walked in on a Monday morning to a phone call from a student's father. This kid had significant GI issues. It was really bad. So bad, in fact, that there were some days where the poor kid spent a good part of his time on the toilet. One particular day, out of sheer concern, we tallied 1 3 trips to the bathroom. You might be thinking, "Wait! There's no way someone can go poo that many times in one day! It has to be task avoidance!" But in fact, he did go poo pretty much every time he was in there because the smell was horrifying, and permeated the hallway and our classroom. We often had to clear the class and go to early recess or take a "brain break" because the smell was so awful. He was even hospitalized for this as they tried to figure out the issue, because it became so pervasive and problematic. He also managed to clog the toilet about eight times in one school year. At times, it got to the point where the school district had to send out maintenance to snake the line to unclog the plumbing.

Anyhow, upon answering the phone on this fateful Monday morning, the father proceeded to tell me that there were some significant issues with his son over the weekend. According to dad, it all began that Friday afternoon when the student got home from school complaining to his parents that his "coconuts were hurting really bad." So upon inspection, his mother found that his nether region was caked in dried up poop, and after cleaning him up properly, his "coconuts" were now red and raw, and he was in a lot of pain. His dad had called to let me know that my student, his son, would be coming to school with wipes and diaper cream. He then proceeded to ask if I would help him and make sure he cleaned himself up after he used the restroom, and if I could "help put diaper cream on his coconuts." *Did I mention this kid was in the 4th grade?* I told his father that it was a hard no and apologized for the inconvenience. When the student asked me himself to help with his "coconuts" I had him retrieve his baby wipes and diaper cream from his bag and asked another student to walk him down to the nurse's office to ask for her help. I don't know what happened after that, but I was never able to wipe the image of the poop encrusted, red and raw coconuts from my mind.

WALDO'S DAD NEEDS GAS MONEY

To: Waldo's father
From: Waldo's teacher
Subject: Appt. Confirmation
Good morning,
I just wanted to confirm our appointment for after school today. We will be discussing Waldo's grades and attendance.
Thank you.

To: Waldo's teacher
From: Waldo's father
Subject: Re: Appt. Confirmation
Yeah I'll be there today but my check didn't come in yesterday so do you think you could loan me $20 for gas money?

MY STUDENT VAMPIRINA

ANONYMOUS

ONE OF MY STUDENTS WAS ALREADY KNOWN FOR SOME bad behaviors. She would cut class, drink alcohol at school, etc. She would come to class and tell teachers to fuck off, or just not do anything at all. She was a real treat.

One day my admin asked me to "chat with her to see if she is okay or not" and as soon as I sat down beside her she was super fidgety and saying bizarre things. She asked me if I loved to cut and if I wanted to cut right now, and by cut I do *not* mean skip school. She wanted to draw her own blood. I kept asking her what she was on, because it was clear she was not sober, and she would just giggle like a little troll. I was able to get her to admit that she had snorted Gravol (also known as Dramamine), which apparently causes psychotropic effects such as hallucinations. Admin never came to check on us, and I felt trapped there with her. Clearly she couldn't be left alone.

Suddenly she yelled, "I'm going to get some water!" and then sprinted like a gremlin down the hall. I called after her but she kept going so I followed her. She moved very quickly, turned a corner and was out of sight. I followed her, upping my pace, and when I turned the corner she was standing in a doorway, cutting the shit out of herself with a huge blade. There was blood everywhere. She was cutting with reckless abandon, just slicing and dicing. I yelled at her to give me the blade, but she just ran away from me, continuing to cut herself. I didn't know what to do and I was genuinely concerned that she would cut too deeply, so I body slammed her into a locker and wrestled the blade out of her hand (which ended up being a broken steak knife). Then she started to suck her own blood. She did not just take a couple of licks, but was fully sucking it back like a vampire. She glared at me with a mouth full of blood dripping from her teeth.

I took her by the arm and dragged her to the office. They sent her home with her mother. I was sent to my next class, and given no time to process the whole event. I was told to tell absolutely no one that this had occurred. The student came back to school the next day and acted like nothing had happened. I was never checked on by admin and the staff was never told that this had happened.

YOU RUINED HER CHILDHOOD

To: *8th* **grade English teacher**
CC: Principal
From: Angry parent
Subject: Ruined Childhood

We have had a very rough weekend at our home.
It started with Shangela getting in the car on
Friday afternoon after chorus practice. She
said, "My English teacher ruined my childhood
today," and started sobbing. She explained that
you announced to the class that Santa is not real
and that parents do all of the magic themselves
and have more fun than the kids.
Aside from Shangie being tenderhearted and
hurt by your comments, my concern is why you
would think it is okay to say something like
that. Why is it okay to make a generalized state-
ment about a belief, not knowing who might
actually have that belief? I hope you don't make

**other statements about other cultures that
might conflict with a student's belief.
My daughter has lost a big chunk of her inno-
cence and I don't know how to ease this for her.**

(*NOTE: Shangie is fourteen years old.*)

I SAY A LITTLE PRAYER FOR YOU

ANONYMOUS

LAST YEAR I HAD A STUDENT ENROLLED IN MY CLASS who had just been released from a behavioral hospital. He was in the program since kindergarten and was finally being integrated back into the public school system in third grade. He was sent to my classroom in November, and I immediately noticed something wasn't right. He was taller than me. I'm under five feet but it is rare for a third grader to be taller than me. I checked his file, and he was held back twice in the behavioral school. Keep in mind that I am just a general education classroom teacher with no training in special education or behavioral issues.

The student was extremely violent and continuously thought that everyone was out to get him. He got into a fight with someone when we were hanging up our jackets after recess. The student bumped into him, and he proceeded to take the student's head and repeatedly bash it into the floor until security came into my room to break it up.

He was given two days of out of school suspension, but he was gone for another two weeks after that. When he finally came back from school, he was wearing four crucifix necklaces. I asked him where he had been for the last two and a half weeks, and this is where the story gets wild.

He told me that he had an exorcism and was recovering from that. I asked him what he meant by that. He said that his mom told him that Satan was living inside him, and that is why he was acting out. She completely dismissed the fact that he was formally diagnosed with schizophrenia. His mom took him into the basement of a church, and there were lit candles everywhere. A woman in the basement had him lie down on a table, and they proceeded to get the demon out of him by throwing holy water at him and screaming prayers.

He also told me that the woman gave his demon a name and told him that if he needed to, he could call the demon back into his body. I asked what the name of the demon was, but he didn't want to tell me for fear of calling it back into him. The guidance counselor called home, and his mom confirmed the story.

For the rest of the year, the student, who was extremely explosive to begin with, also now believed that he had the ability to summon a demon when he needed one. His behavior got more extreme, and he had a scapegoat of sorts. "It wasn't me! It was the demon!" he would say. He also believed that when his left eye twitched (which happened often), it meant that the devil was near, and we were all in danger.

I was never a religious person, but I did a devotional and read a bible verse every day before work, just to be sure.

FLIPPING STUDENTS THE BIRD

ANONYMOUS

THERE IS A FINE LINE BETWEEN BEING A TEACHER AND being a friend to your students. Sometimes, we are around our students so much that this line gets a little blurry. Such was the case with one of my favorite students, I'll call her Fern. Now, Fern was not a "good" student. She would walk into my fourth period physics class late every day and proclaim, "I hate this class!" I would respond with shock and disappointment, and she would assure me, "No, Ms. P. It's not *you* I hate, it's just this *class*. You're cool." I never got too worked up about her entrances because she usually went to her seat after that and didn't cause much more trouble.

One day she walked in late as usual, but for some reason, she did not want to go to her seat that day–she wanted to stand there and antagonize me. I was trying to get the class started on their day's activities–and she was just purposefully annoying me–asking me questions, talking over me, etc. She was distracting the entire class and found herself to be hilarious. (It was sort of funny at first but went on too long.) After politely telling her to stop multiple times, repeatedly motioning for her to go to her seat, and then ignoring her for about five minutes, I was visibly frustrated. My frustration only amused her more, and she started to ramp up her routine.

So I flipped her off. Full on, in front of the entire class, I gave her the finger. She was the kind of student who wouldn't actually get offended by this, we had a decent relationship, and I knew she would think it was funny. And she did. However, the best part of this for her was the fact that her friend got it on camera. I guess I was so consumed with trying to do my job that I didn't notice she was filming me. She played it back, and there I was, standing in front of my class, flipping off a student.

I asked the student to delete it in front of me, and she did, but somehow it made its way onto the school's social media and became a pretty big sensation amongst the students. They started to use it as a meme, and it just wouldn't go away. Admin never seemed to find out about it, luckily. But even four years later, I am no longer at that school, and a new coworker sent me the video with a bunch of laughing emojis. I just know that any day now, a student will discover my little video, and it will become a phenomenon all over again.

151

SHIT PARENTS SAY

J. MORRIS

THE FOLLOWING IS A COLLECTION OF REAL COMMENTS made by students' parents:

"I hate this school. All these teachers calling me and annoying me all the damn time!" (*Her daughter was failing every class.*)

"You're worse than a drug dealer wanting money!" (*Parent to her son's special education case manager who was trying to schedule a meeting to get him much needed help.*)

"You took my son outside and now he's sick. Are *you* gonna take him to the doctor and pay the bill?"

"Please email me every time my son is not behaving in

class." *After a week of receiving daily emails*: "Don't contact me anymore. I can't control what he does at school."

"I leave my voicemail box full so the school can't leave me messages."

"I think my son is misbehaving because he is sexually frustrated and embarrassed that he is still a virgin."

"From 7:45 to 3 he's your problem. If he shits on the floor because you won't let him go to the bathroom, that's your problem too!"

"My son came home yesterday with very soiled underwear because he doesn't like to poop at school. Could you encourage him to use the potty when he has to poop? He takes a long time because he takes off all of his clothes and squats on top of the toilet seat. Maybe you can explain that he shouldn't do it like that?"

"I understand that my son is in in-school suspension but if he doesn't have pizza for lunch he gets very angry. It will only make things worse. Please pick up his pizza delivery from the front office at 11:30."

"Teachers are one of her triggers. Don't talk to her and try not to make eye contact."

"He would never let me take his phone away."

"We'll be on vacation for the next month. Will she miss anything?"

"Next time there is a school event, please call to let me know. I'm too busy to check his folder every night."

"He didn't cheat. He tells me everything. He said he didn't do it."

"I told him to hit back. I ain't raising no punk!"

"She is only acting that way because she is bored."

"I don't call you on the weekends to complain because that's *your* time. So don't call me during school hours because that's *my* time!"

"My daughter really wants to join your knitting club but it meets when she has dance class. If you can't meet on a different day, can you meet with her during lunch or after school to give her lessons?"

"When will you update your gradebook with all of the assignments she said she did? She should have an A."

"You are the adult. Make him do his work!"

"He's failing because you aren't challenging him enough!"

"Technically I'm your boss. I pay taxes and that pays your salary. I can have you fired whenever I want."

"He stays up all night playing video games. I just don't know what to do about it."

"I'm going to need you to tell me what exactly your credentials are for teaching this class."

"She got lice from *your* dirty classroom!"

Teacher: "Your son is constantly inappropriate."
Mother: "Please give me an example."
Teacher: "Today the students were asked what career they are interested in. He yelled out, 'I want to be a gynecologist and eat fish tacos all day long!'"
Mother: "Well if he wants to be a gynecologist, he'll be the best one out there! Why would you stifle his dream?"

"Are you implying that my son ditches school? He does not! I just let him stay home whenever he wants."

"What exactly do you mean by 'strangled?' Did he apply pressure?"

Teacher: "Your son will not stop talking while I'm teaching."
Parent: "Yeah well we all have parts of our job that we don't like."

"She said you don't like her."

"He says he didn't do it and I believe him."

152

COMMITMENT

RANDALL MUCKENTHALLER

I AM A SPECIAL ED. CO-TEACHER IN A FIFTH GRADE inclusion classroom. I had a really rough year last year due to a toxic work environment that took a shot at my confidence as a teacher. The year started off with us getting the heads up that I would have a boy (I'll call Herb) who is nonverbal autistic, and has a device he uses to communicate. Nobody had been able to get him to communicate with them with his device outside of his family.

I met with the family, and they were fantastic. The mom told me that Herb communicated with her and his dad with his device, but he is very shy about using it in front of others, so I shouldn't take it personally. Throughout the day, I did everything in my power to communicate with him, figure out how to make his day the best it could possibly be, and just tried to make him feel comfortable. He was very irritable and I had to follow him all around the school because he would continuously need to leave and go for walks.

Finally, at the end of the day, we were sitting on the bench when his mom came. She took out the device and asked him if he wanted to say anything to me, and he surprisingly said yes! His mom was immediately surprised since she said he had never said yes before. He started typing for about five minutes and then showed us the message. It said, "i loved your cammitment mr n and we are doing great because you care about me." It took everything in my power not to cry because of how incredible this was on top of the fact that his mom started to get emotional because she said he had never done anything like that before. Then he put his head on my shoulder and typed that he didn't want to leave.

If I could point to one moment in my entire teaching career that solidified my drive to continue teaching and my teaching philosophy that every child can learn and reach their fullest potential with the proper support and care, this one was it.

CONTAIN THIS SHIT!

It was March of 2020, and humanity was going about its business and suddenly we all had to stay home for, like, *ever*. But school has to continue somehow and parents have a huge task ahead of them.

Teachers sat back and waited for parents to realize how hard our job is. We waited for the praise, and the outpouring of appreciation. And a bit of that did happen. Parents made funny videos showing their newfound gratitude, such as comedian Wayne Colley, who says to his child's teacher, "I'd like to thank you for everything you have done with my child this year. I didn't know that you teachers had it so hard and you are a hero to me," as he sheds a few tears. British comedian Judi Love screams, "I don't understand how you keep them entertained for six hours straight! I can't do it for two hours! We love you! Some of you teachers are not just teachers, you're also parents, social workers, general practitioners, nurses, counselors, police officers. We're sorry and we're going to appreciate you so much more!" Comedian Doug Williams hid in his car and exclaimed into his phone, "We got to get rid of this virus so we can open these schools back up! I'm trying to do this homeschooling... All I got to say is *pay the mutha-fuckin teachers*! You have made a believer out of me! There's no reason teachers shouldn't be making as much as doctors and lawyers cuz they have to deal with 30 of these muthafuckas at one time! They are like 30 muthafuckin viruses walking through your classroom every day! Damn the homeless! We don't need money for the homeless! They had their chance! Raise more money for the teachers! Teachers need to be tipped like waitresses. If you know your child is out of control, you need to send a tip every day to the muthafuckin teacher! *Everybody* try to come up with a cure! *We got to send these kids back to school!"*

But my favorite video was made by an unknown mom, who also escaped to her car to film her rant which included, "I had to come into this muthafuckin car to get away from these muthafuckin kids. Listen here Trunk. I don't know what the fuck going on, but whatever y'all put into this air, y'all need to *contain* this shit! Because these muthafuckas need to go back to school! These muthafuckas can't go to school, these bitches can't go to the beach, and they can't go to the muthafuckin trampoline place! I'm tryna figure out what the fuck is it that y'all want us to do with these mutha-fuckin kids! I'm used to my kids being in school Trunk! *Contain this shit!"* (Google "Listen Here Trunk" for the full rant.)

There were a lot of tweets applauding teachers that went viral as well such as, "2.5 hours into homeschooling my kids: Teachers need to make more than professional athletes, CEOs, and all of Hollywood combined," and, "Teachers are some of the mentally strongest people on earth."

But a lot of people were not satisfied with the level of

remote learning that teachers were providing. Just look at these comments:

"What are teachers doing? I assume they are getting paid in full. Why aren't towns putting teachers to work, cleaning stuff, and picking up trash, anything to better the community that is paying them to sit home and do nothing?"

"There are teachers in the country that are being paid to go biking and hiking. Open those schools back up and get to work!"

"THIS IS NOT A VACATION FOR YOU TEACHERS!!! I am not sure what situations other parents have, but I am working a full time job at home and you just get to send out an assignment and say, 'Here students! Have at it!' That is BULLSHIT!!!"

"Does anyone know if state and federal funding is available for parents for homeschooling? If schools are shut down and we aren't working then these funds should be available to us, right?"

"I have expressed my concerns that we are now doing the teachers' work without compensation. This is illegal. I requested stipends for parents and I will start a petition. No more full salary! I lost it yesterday when my special needs teachers sent me a book on video and told me what to do. I said I AM NOT DOING YOUR WORK WITHOUT COMPENSATION! They need to adjust teachers' salaries and make available funds for parents for our efforts."

"Teachers are basically just home collecting a paycheck

while the parents work full time, educate our kids, and pay taxes? That's not right!"

"We are using our homes as classrooms and our taxes pay for education! I'm calling the mayor's office because we need to get a check for teachers staying at home and doing nothing! My wife and I are doing their jobs! I want my money back!"

"Zero homeschooling going on in my home. Until they start making the assignments mandatory, I will not be giving them any schoolwork to do. I don't get paid for that."

Okay, so that last lady is just like, "Fuck this, my kids can be ignorant, there's no way I'm interacting with them," but at least she's not coming for our checks! So many people think we're just chilling at home, collecting a paycheck. But the reality is, most teachers are working harder than ever, with little to no resources, and have their own families to take care of, *at the same time.*

And some of the expectations are insane. Administrators in Madison, Wisconsin made the news when they emailed their teachers and informed them that they "cannot watch (their) children and work at the same time." They said, "The expectation is that you secure childcare. Whether the childcare is outside of your home or in your home is up to you." That kind of goes against the whole social distancing thing, doesn't it? After a huge backlash on social media they changed their message to, "Plan ahead as much as possible for childcare in your home so that interruptions are minimized."

Many schools are insisting that teachers maintain a presence online for seven or more hours a day to earn their paychecks. One teacher emailed her administrator and said, "I am really worried that I won't be able to maintain seven hours a day on my computer while caring for my three-month-old and two-year-old. My husband is considered an emergency worker and will not be home to help. I have set up plans for my students to complete work independently, which I will update and grade daily. But I won't be able to be a good mom if I have to be at the computer all day." And her admin responded, "I understand it might be a pain. Unfortunately, we have to stay consistent and do the same practices. You must still log in at the same time every morning and stay on Zoom for the entire workday. Let your students know that they may hear screaming and crying in the background. Kids will understand and parents will too."

Schools are not only having teachers "teaching" online for seven or more hours, they are also making them attend numerous virtual meetings before and after the school day, and some even on the weekend. Despite all of the planning and time that will go into this new form of teaching, many teachers were also told that any work that students complete is for "enrichment" and cannot actually count towards their grade.

Some school administrators just refuse to let their teachers stay home. Even when it became mandated by each state to close the schools, many teachers were still required to come to school to do work, watch sick kids, or even *clean* the school. Here are some quotes from administrative emails that were passed on to me:

"Please note that employees will have to provide a doctor's note specifying that they have to self-quarantine. Otherwise, attendance will count against your allotment of days."

"Be calm for the students. It is much safer for them here at school than out in crowded areas. Keep the conversations positive and do not cause them undue stress."

"To clarify, we are *not* closing school. We will be having regular school days on Mondays, Wednesdays, and Fridays. On Tuesdays and Thursdays, the teachers are expected to report to work as usual and clean the building to make it safe for students to attend. We understand that some of you are considered high risk, and you will need to use your sick days and then take unpaid leave. These are historic times, and we all need to be team players."

"School is closed for students but not for teachers. If your own children also do not have school, you cannot bring them here."

"Today's communication talked about the electronic delivery of the curriculum, but it did *not* state that faculty and staff would be working virtually. We expect all faculty and staff to be on campus. I am hoping we can instill a spirit of confidence and optimism for our students. I see this as a great adventure and spot on with what we have called forward in our strategic plan for the future. Who knew that we would encounter the future so soon! Have a great day and let students know you look forward to seeing them virtually soon!"

"Tomorrow students will begin their online learning program. Teachers are to report to school as usual in professional attire and conduct online classes according to a schedule. Let's make online learning awesome!"

"Please report to the cafeteria tomorrow at 8 AM for curriculum planning. Please dress professionally."

"When we begin virtual learning, you will be expected to work FROM SCHOOL while students tune in from home. If daycare is closed, you may bring your children with a pack & play if needed."

"At the end of every day, staff needs to send a report to the administration outlining the work they completed, and the time it took to complete it. This report needs to include students who are not responding and actions taken. If any staff member defaults from these duties, then they will be required to work from school. Administration may stop a staff member from working from home at their discretion."

"During a virtual drop-in observation today an administrator observed a kindergarten lesson. They could see several wine bottles on the counter behind the teacher. Please be cognizant that others can see into your teaching space and be aware of professionalism in your setting."

"Teachers must document and log every time there is an interaction with a student or parent. You are expected to respond to all school related communication in a timely manner from 8 AM to 8 PM."

Veteran middle school teacher Justin Parmenter wrote a piece for the Charlotte Observer about how overwhelmed he is with the expectations put on him as a teacher, and as a parent to two elementary aged children. "I would be expected to be at my laptop physically teaching live classes via video conference from 8 a.m. to 3 p.m. every day, including office hours during lunch. The burden of trying to adapt everything I'd be doing in a physical classroom to an online format, manage my own kids' learning throughout the day, handle an insane amount of communication and do it all with the added stress of living under a deadly pandemic came crashing down on me. *I can't &$#@ing do this anymore*, I thought to myself. *This is not sustainable."*

A large majority of school districts have agreed that it isn't fair to assign grades for work done during the pandemic, due to varying issues such as access to technology. Parents are overwhelmed trying to keep up with their children's schoolwork while working full time, and meanwhile, it really is only assigned "for enrichment." Teachers are not inundating students and parents with messages and work because we *want* to, or because we think it's what's best for kids and their families. We are doing it to earn our paychecks, because that is what we were instructed to do.

As if the expectations for keeping up with online teaching weren't enough, admin started doing observations online. They would just pop in unannounced to do formal write-ups. A teacher sent me a form that is used to formally evaluate her online teaching. The categories include how well the teacher managed the chat, conveyed lesson objectives, used different learning platforms, used differentiation, used various resources, different forms of assessment to ensure students "mastered the learning objective," fostered critical thinking, varied explanations, managed student behavior, encouraged participation, and actively engaged students. Admins planned on popping in to her online learning sessions to assess her based on this criteria. On a normal school day, this is perhaps reasonable though still asking for *a lot*. During the current circumstances? Pure, unadulterated, insensitive, insane *horseshit*. Does it matter to admin whether or not a student puts a cardboard cutout of Danny DeVito in their place during their Zoom session? Would the teacher be docked for their pantsless toddler eating three crayons in the background of their Google Meet session? Would points be deducted for a student hacking into the learning platform and playing porn?

Think that's bullshit? How about the fact that some schools actually required their teachers to conduct fire drills from home, asking them to take photos of themselves and their families outside as evidence? Even worse than that is the amendment to the teachers' contract that one district sent out for teachers to sign. It said that teachers were expected to be on the clock from 8 AM to 8 PM, and secondary teachers were expected to call students' homes a *minimum* of three times per week (for secondary teachers, this can be up to 200 students). It was implied that if they did not sign, they might not have a job next year.

I just couldn't believe what I was hearing. Everyday a teacher would send me some insane request they received from their admin. An interesting little idea that many schools came up with to get students pumped for online learning was a "Distance Learning Staff Pride Parade." They asked teachers (some even *required* it), to decorate their cars and join them in a line as they drove through their students' neighborhoods and yelled and honked their horns. *Woo.*

Parent messages to teachers have been absolute gems.

Some parents had ridiculous requests and wanted help parenting their own kids:

"Anyways can I can get reimbursed for all the paper and ink we're using?" (*LOL lady! Welcome to our world!*)

I'm so disappointed of him right know

Can you please talk to him

He justa want to watch tv
play Nintendo

Would you be able to call me and talk to her? My
number is ~~████████~~ I just told her to get up to
do her work and she refused.

Ms. L   told me
that tomorrow there will be
homeschool again, I would
like to ask if I could record for
the channel on YouTube, I will
not show the children it would
be just you, I believe that
         's subscribers would
love to watch
Thank you

Some just gave up:

's parent

N████ is going to fail I don't
understand science or ss

Hi it's Mrs
    If I can
help in any way
please let me
3:49 PM   know!!

Just help me
uninroll them. I
can't do this.   3:50 PM

Some were quite rude:

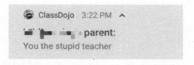

ClassDojo 3:22 PM ∧

▄▆ ▄▆ ▄▆ parent:
You the stupid teacher

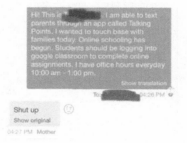

Hello Mrs ████████ would email or FaceTime work better for you for ████████ receiving OT? If email, could you text it to me

No

Ok no problem. Thanks

Hi! This is ████████ I am able to text parents through an app called Talking Points. I wanted to touch base with families today. Online schooling has begun. Students should be logging into google classroom to complete online assignments. I have office hours everyday 10:00 am – 1:00 pm.

Show translation

To: ████████ 04:26 PM

Shut up
Show original
04:27 PM Mother

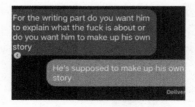

For the writing part do you want him to explain what the fuck is about or do you want him to make up his own story

He's supposed to make up his own story

Deliver

Some were really starting to appreciate their kids' teachers:

And again they do not pay you guys enough. I threw a towel at him earlier to get his attention!

Question 🙂🙂 how did you even get to teach ▓▓▓▓ 😕 😦 this kid don't even let me get a word in 😩😩 he has a story for everythinggggggg 😩. After one day I'm ready to quit, now I could just imagine you oohh lord!! I have to pray for you everyday smh I didn't know it was this bad omg we don't give teachers enough credit and I'm sorry you have to deal with our children everyday!! Be safe & thank you again

▓▓▓▓▓ I know this is your work email account, but do you have to drink to get through ▓▓▓▓ essays!?! Helping him edit his essay was near torture and we only got a 1/3 of the way through before he no longer wanted my help. There were tears, from him too, and I'm not sure what is going to be handed in the end but we worked on it the best we could and we will continue to do so tonight and tomorrow! God bless you! ▓▓▓▓

And some just let it all out:

My academically unmotivated child wants to
know if she still has to do her homework packet
since the world is ending? It's interfering
with her Tik Tok videos and multiple views of
Dance Moms reruns. I told her yes, of course
she has to do it; but I'm an idiot and don't know
what I'm talking about. She needs to hear it
from you. Also, do you know if there will be
anything done online for the end of the year
since we have no end in sight to this shutdown?

Re: Earth Science: Progress Reports
Today at 9:00 PM

Why???....Why???.... Is this child ⬛⬛⬛⬛
now saying....after all we went through
earlier today.....he is now saying that he
doesn't know what website to go on.....to get
words and definitions to make flashcards.
Why???...I promise you, I only smoked one lil
piece of a blunt before I even knew I was
pregnant with him. It wasn't enough to mess
him up like this. I promise you. I don't know
what to do with this child.

And the students? How were they handling this whole online schooling scenario? Well, two different school districts reported that students had recorded their teachers during online classes and either turned the audio into hate speech or turned the visual into pornography, which circulated on social media. Others protested the work very openly and just let it all fly with their opinions, while some engaged in totally inappropriate yet rather entertaining conversations.

High quality student work:

I want to shar my brotr brot home a baby racon and thot it was a baby dog but it was a baby ratcon so we toc care of it and let it free

1. GREATEST DESSERT EVER?

DEEZ NUTZ

F*** english!

Teacher thinks she's SOOO smart. B*llsh*t she's a pain in the ass that thinks the obvious isn't obvious. Dumbass. She is like,"Oh! Let's have them work on their info books strike 1. Resays what everyone is already thinking, strike 2. What if you have and are waiting for a teacher to check it? (The revised chapter.) Then what!? Strike 3. And she forgot to mention this MIGHT help, MIGHT.Doesn't help me in any way, shape, or form.Strike 4 & 5.Your out!

Open Protests:

I made a few comments on your document and returned it to you to look over. No need to resubmit, this was great for your first time trying out a hyperdoc! :)

leave me alone

12:06 PM

this trash i hope all the teachers catch corona

Ain't nobody got time to wake up at a certain time to finish work. Th? I'm tryna sleep till 1pm my guy. Not finish stupid English work 😩😩 leave me and my coronacation aloonnneeeeee 😤😤😵😵

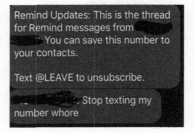

Remind Updates: This is the thread for Remind messages from You can save this number to your contacts.

Text @LEAVE to unsubscribe.

Stop texting my number whore

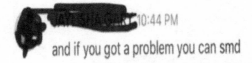

yoo this shit got my brain hurtin im not doin this shit

10:44 PM

and if you got a problem you can smd

"this assingment makes me wanna go outside and lick a subway pole then cough on a kid"

REPLY

: comments

stop posting mad work

stooooooooooooooooooooooooooooooooooo
oooooooooooooooooooooooooooooooooooo
oooooooooooooooooooooooooooooooooooo
oooooooooooooooooooooooooppppppppppppp
pppppppppppppppppppppppppppppppppppppp
pppppppppppppppppppppppppppppppppppp
ppppppppppppppppppppppppppppppppppppp
ppppppppppppppppppppppp

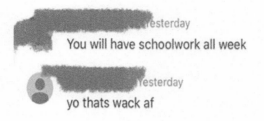

You will have schoolwork all week

yo thats wack af

I shared my google doc with you. i dont drink but after that project i need me something strong. i feel like somebody just gave me a lobotomy with the biggest dildo they could find.

"First off who are
u talking to ?!
And how u going
to tell me if I did
the actual after
the video ?! I did
do the
predictions boo
have a nice day

Subject: Re: A Reflection from Mr. H

marry a wife already

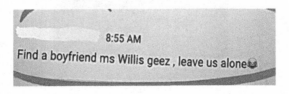

"I dont think its
possible for me to
do such a
assignment and if
you think im
dressing up then you
must be high"

Others made some strange comments in the class chats:

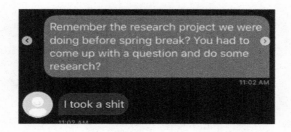

> Remember the research project we were doing before spring break? You had to come up with a question and do some research?
>
> 11:02 AM
>
> I took a shit
>
> 11:02 AM

Class comments

  **n** Yesterday

I have done number 1 in my pance and my parents aren't home and I have rolled around in it for 3 hours

Please be sure to log into these pages everyday
and devote some time and effort into the
assignments.

---

2 class comments

 7:06 AM

ok mr . penis man

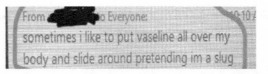

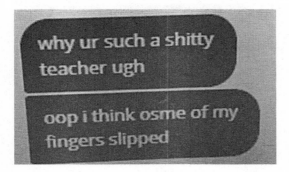

Ms. ⬛ :11 AM
I will post a link and you click on it and that's about it. I still need everyone to add the google classroom first.

Brandon ⬛ 6:45 PM
Johnnnnnn

John ⬛ 6:51 PM
Brandonnn

Brandon ⬛ 6:53 PM
How've you been John

John 7:12 PM
Good shit has been wack staying home I am trying to go blaze it how you been

Brandon Yesterday
Bruh I feel you always be stressing sometimes just gotta take a blinker from a stizzy rq. I've been good straight chillin everyday with the boys

John Yesterday
Fax and smoke a couple of blunts

Brandon Yesterday
Sleep hella good

And they came up with some rather creative screen names as well:

Most teachers who are required to conduct live online classes are using *Zoom*, a video conferencing app. Many businesses and community groups are using it as well. It is currently used by 32 million people per day. It's a pretty useful tool where the whole class can see each other and interact online at the same time. However, hackers quickly figured out how to sit in on meetings, gathering private information and other sensitive material. Some brilliant people figured out how to post a loop of themselves so they would not actually have to attend a meeting (which I wouldn't mind at all for PLCs, etc.) Then the term "zoom bombing" was coined. This refers to hackers joining a zoom meeting and taking over by displaying hate speech or even pornography. There have been kindergarten classes who have learned about some very adult things during their homeschooling. If anyone asks why I never held live classes, this will be my number one reason!

So that's currently where we're at. It's the sixth week of quarantine and I suppose at this point I'm just resigned to it. I've got an elementary aged kid and a toddler. I'm trying my best to help the older one with schoolwork. As for the toddler, we're just keeping her alive at this point. Not a whole lot of enrichment other than "Toddler Learning Videos" on YouTube. Just being honest. There's only so much I'm capable of... and teaching full time and teaching the older one, and trying to keep them off screens at least *some* of the time, along with all the household shit... I'm not a fucking superhero or a machine. I'm not that good at the house shit to begin with. Now it's just a straight-up shit show.

I'm lucky to be in a district that isn't requiring specific hours or live teaching. I just post work and grade it. And only about half of the kids are doing it. Normally that bothers me but the reduced workload is helping me be able to function. I love my kids and I had them on purpose and everything but holy shit, this is too much. The toddler is such a fucking toddler. Her favorite words are NO and MINE and if those don't work she just shrieks. That's her main mode of communication: shrieking. She has a decent vocabulary for a two-year-old but screeching is so much more effective. People all around you will swoop in immediately to figure out what you want. I think I might try this. I admire her preschool teachers so much. *They deal with like twelve of these fuckers at a time.* But they seem to enjoy it for the most part. I guess it's how outsiders view middle school and high school teachers. Like woah, you *choose* to hang out with those kids every day?

I want to end this with something super insightful but I'm so tired and worn out I'm not sure that what I'm saying is even coherent. I keep telling myself *it's just a moment in time, you'll look back one day and laugh,* as I stare in the dirty bathroom mirror and pop another Xanax. I keep drinking way too much coffee in the morning to be able to handle all this shit and then I get super anxious and irrational and start screaming at everyone and shaking. That's when those helpful pills come into play. And I'm so much less likely to murder someone.

Let's just hope that when this whole thing is over people in general will hold on to a new appreciation for teachers. Maybe when they start typing out an angry email about their precious child and how they couldn't possibly be at fault for *anything ever* they'll think back to this time and recall what it was like to spend all fucking day with that kid. Hopefully they'll click delete and go buy a Starbucks gift card instead!

Thank you for reading, and thank you for your reviews. Your support and feedback are the best gifts you can give an author. Please rate on Amazon and Goodreads!

Thank you friend,
Jane Morris

ACKNOWLEDGEMENTS

When I first started teaching I was like, "Okay. This shit is fucking crazy. This is not at all what I expected. This is insane. There's no way I can keep doing this." So I actually told myself that I was going to use writing to get myself out. I started writing down all the stories, all the crazy bullshit that I couldn't let go of. Every time something awful happened I comforted myself with the idea that it was just more material to write about, and make jokes about on social media.

I kept chasing this dream... and I am lucky enough to have a husband who, instead of telling me that maybe what I was doing wasn't a good idea, kept pushing and saying KEEP GOING! Things gained momentum. I published my first book *Teacher Misery*. It sold way more copies than I ever could have imagined! People related to my stories. I wasn't just telling MY story... I was painting a picture of just how much teaching has changed and how absurd it is. I kept teaching, so I had more stories. I wrote another book called *More Teacher Misery*. I was so worried that it wouldn't live up to the first, but all the feedback was amazing!

I'm still writing. I'm having fun. I'm letting go, knowing that wherever I take you all, you'll support it! I'm still teaching because of you, my readers, and because of this outlet. This is my therapy, and your support means more than you can know! We're a miserable little family, and only *we* know what it's really like, and why we keep showing up for more, despite it all.

So thank you, my readers and followers, for supporting me and giving me a voice!

Thank you to everyone who contributed to this book and everyone who submitted a story. You are brave!

Thank you to my closest work comrades (B.P., C.L., M.G.) who know who I really am and why I write my books. You know that despite how much I complain, I still love teaching and my students. You get me.

Thanks Mia D. for editing this one!

Thanks Mom for dealing with my over-the-top teenage angst, letting me make mistakes and take risks. Sorry I was always the old lady and never the princess in the school plays. But half of my comedic weirdness comes from you, so it's partially your fault.

Thanks to my kids, who are way too little to understand my sarcasm, but take it all in stride. You're helping me learn how to let go a little, which I've been needing to do for a long, long time.

Thank you to my husband, for understanding when I get that spark and need to drop everything and write, even when you have to take over everything. And thanks for letting me sleep way more than you. That's true love.

NOTES

4. Popsicle Disservice

1. PBIS stands for *Positive Behavioral Interventions and Supports.* The idea is that you mostly ignore negative behavior and reward positive behavior.

11. The World's Shittiest Gifts

1. *Yes, that's a real book. No, I haven't read it. Yes, I kinda want to. If you really need a laugh, check out the other titles by the same author, Dr. Chuck Tingle. Do you think he's a real doctor?*
2. *I know I'm shitting on admin quite a bit in this section, so let me just say that some admins are awesome, okay? Here I'm talking about the ones that seem to get off on making our lives hell. You know those dicks. Those are exactly the type who would give you a snow globe with their fucking faces in it.*

132. Morning Cocktail

1. *Lean*, also known as *purple drank*, is a combination of prescription-strength cough medicine, soft drinks, and hard, fruit-flavored candy.

ABOUT THE AUTHOR

Jane Morris is the pen name of a teacher who just wants to tell the truth without losing her job. She has taught English for over 15 years in a major American city. It is her dream to write comedy full time. So if you have any ideas, contact her so she can finally show her face!

She received her B.A. in English and Secondary Education from a well-known university. She earned her M.A. in Writing from an even fancier (more expensive) university. She loves dogs, trees and other things that can't talk. She has a loving family and cares about making people laugh more than anything else.

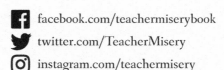

facebook.com/teachermiserybook

twitter.com/TeacherMisery

instagram.com/teachermisery